US SUPREME COURT LANDMARK CASES

A WOMAN'S RIGHT TO AN ABORTION
Roe v. Wade

D. J. HERDA

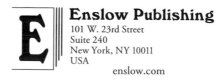

Enslow Publishing
101 W. 23rd Street
Suite 240
New York, NY 10011
USA

enslow.com

Published in 2017 by Enslow Publishing, LLC.
101 W. 23rd Street, Suite 240, New York, NY 10011

Library of Congress Cataloging-in-Publication Data

Names: Herda, D. J., 1948–, author.
Title: A woman's right to an abortion : Roe v. Wade / D. J. Herda.
Description: New York, NY : Enslow Publishing, LLC, 2017. | Series: US Supreme Court landmark cases | Includes bibliographical references and index.
Identifiers: LCCN 2016024486 | ISBN 9780766084247 (library bound)
Subjects: LCSH: Roe, Jane, 1947—Trials, litigation, etc.—Juvenile literature. | Wade, Henry—Trials, litigation, etc.—Juvenile literature. | Trials (Abortion)—United States—Juvenile literature. | Abortion—Law and legislation—United States—Juvenile literature.
Classification: LCC KF228.R59 H473 2017 | DDC 342.7308/4—dc23 LC record available at https://lccn.loc.gov/2016024486

Printed in Malaysia

To Our Readers: We have done our best to make sure all websites in this book were active and appropriate when we went to press. However, the author and the publisher have no control over and assume no liability for the material available on those websites or on any websites they may link to. Any comments or suggestions can be sent by e-mail to customerservice@enslow.com.

Portions of this book originally appeared in the book *Roe v. Wade: The Abortion Question.*

Contents

CHAPTER 1

Dallas, Texas

As Norma McCorvey sat in a small family restaurant on Mockingbird Lane in Dallas, Texas, she cradled her cup of coffee in her hands and sighed. This was not a first for her, but still, she didn't know what to expect. Lawyers had always made her uncomfortable. This day was no different.

But she waited patiently nonetheless for the arrival of Linda Coffee and Sarah Weddington, two attorneys who had set up a meeting with her to discuss her problem. It had all started a few months earlier, in August 1969. McCorvey had a job selling tickets to a carnival sideshow, an animal act that traveled throughout the South. The work was boring, but McCorvey enjoyed it anyway—or rather, she enjoyed the aura of the traveling show. She loved the free-spirited lifestyle that she shared with the others with whom she worked, and she loved

---

This photo of McCorvey was taken in 1987. Despite her case being instrumental in giving women the right to choose an abortion in this country, she would later become an activist for pro-life groups.

the people. For the first time in her life, she felt like she was part of a family.

Her coworkers accepted her for who she was rather than for what she had, or had not, accomplished in life. They placed no demands on her, asked her no questions about her past. She had become especially good friends with two of them, women with whom she shared a small motel room.[1] McCorvey's train of thought was suddenly broken as Linda Coffee entered the restaurant. The woman, a twenty-six-year-old corporate lawyer who looked—and was—all business, was of average height and weight. She wore her hair in a simple bun. She was dressed in a conservative beige suit and had a brusque, no-nonsense manner about her, typical of someone in her line of work. That was one of the things McCorvey immediately liked about her. No nonsense.[2]

The two women, who had met to discuss McCorvey's problem twice before, talked for several minutes—small talk, about the weather, McCorvey's job, subjects such as that. They had just about run out of things to say to one another when a third woman, Sarah Weddington, arrived. Unlike Coffee, Weddington was tall and big-boned with a thick mane of strawberry blonde hair. Her flawless white complexion and deep-set blue eyes were complemented by her flouncy pastel dress. McCorvey liked her, too, even though the only thing the flashier Weddington shared with Coffee was her profession: both were lawyers.

McCorvey breathed in deeply as the women ordered pizza and beer. Then, after the small talk had ended, she began to share her story. Coffee had heard it before. Weddington had heard it, too, secondhand from Coffee. Now it was time for her to hear it from McCorvey's own lips.

McCorvey Tells Her Story

It began, McCorvey said, one hot summer's night as the carnival closed its run in a small town near Augusta, Georgia. A group of rough-looking young men had been hanging around most of the evening, drinking, cursing, and generally trying to cause problems for the workers. It was not the kind of behavior that McCorvey found unusual. Traveling shows often encounter such people, so she thought little more about it.

Following the closing of the show for the night, several hours of work remained to be done. The tents had to be taken down and the equipment packed away so that the carnival could leave town early the next morning. Rather than wait around for their usual ride, McCorvey and her friends decided to walk the short distance to their motel. On the way, McCorvey told the two lawyers, they were attacked and McCorvey was raped. She couldn't remember much about the incident, except that she'd been frightened and confused. When Weddington pressed her for more details, McCorvey said she thought that the man who raped her could have been one of the men who had caused trouble at the carnival earlier that night.[3]

Weddington asked what had happened to the two women who were with McCorvey that night. McCorvey could not recall. She knew only that when she regained her senses, she was alone. She managed to stumble back to her motel room only to find

that her friends had already left, taking all their belongings—
and hers, too—with them. She thought about reporting the
rape, telling someone, *anyone*, about what had happened, but
for some reason she decided against it. Instead, she crawled into
bed and slept fitfully until the early morning sun shone through
the curtains. McCorvey scrambled to her feet and threw on her
clothes. As she peeked out the door, she realized that her worst
fears had come true. The carnival had pulled up stakes and left,
leaving her without a cent to her name.

McCorvey decided to return to Dallas, where her family
and several friends lived. She telephoned one of her friends and
asked her to send enough money for the long bus trip home.
The friend wired the exact fare, no more, and McCorvey had
to swap the motel radio to a taxi driver in exchange for a ride
to the bus station.

When she finally reached Dallas, McCorvey made her way to
her friend's trailer home, where she crawled into bed and slept
for two full days. After she was rested, her friend helped her find
a job as a waitress in a local bar. That's what she'd been doing,
she told the two lawyers, ever since. That's what she'd been doing
when she began to suspect she had a problem.

At first the signs were subtle. Some swelling around her
eyes. Occasional nausea. A missed menstrual period. McCorvey
wrote the signs off as symptoms of stress. She had since left her
friend's trailer and moved around from place to place, stopping
anywhere she could find a spare bed for a night or two. She
eventually moved in with her father, but that did not work for
long. He had recently divorced his wife and was drinking heavily.

Whenever he got drunk, he became abusive. McCorvey decided to move in with still another friend.

As the days turned into weeks, McCorvey's physical symptoms changed. The occasional bouts of nausea became more frequent. She found herself craving foods she had never cared for before. She even began to look different, swollen, the way she had looked years ago when she'd been pregnant with her only daughter. Finally, she went to see a physician.

Yes, he had told her finally, there was no doubt about it. She was pregnant. Those were not words McCorvey needed to hear. What would she do? Where would she go? She had no home, little income, and no idea of who the father was. She couldn't even support her own daughter, who was living at the time with McCorvey's mother and stepfather in Arkansas.

Looking for a Way Out

McCorvey went back to her physician and asked him for information about an abortion, even though abortions in Texas were illegal in 1969, just as they were in most other states. That didn't mean that abortions never took place in Texas. Occasionally, a physician would write out the name of an abortionist on a piece of paper and slip it to his patient. That was the next best thing to an open recommendation, since it implied that the physician believed that the abortionist was at the very least competent. Most Texas physicians, though, refused to get involved with such recommendations. Some lectured their patients about being selfish for not wanting to have a child.

Others tried to reassure their patients that, once the baby was born, their maternal instincts would "kick in," and everything would work out for the best.

McCorvey's physician flatly refused to help. He suggested instead that she move to a state where the abortion laws were more liberal. California and Colorado, two nearby states, had recently legalized abortions, although both states imposed strict residency requirements and length-of-pregnancy rules on abortion applicants that would make it difficult for McCorvey to qualify.

McCorvey had heard that some Texas women had traveled to Mexico to have abortions, but most of the clinics there were unlicensed, and their health and sanitary practices were highly questionable. She quickly decided to reject that alternative. Besides, she had barely enough money to survive, let alone travel around in search of a decent abortion clinic. Her best alternative seemed to be to seek an abortion in Texas—an *illegal* abortion.

McCorvey soon learned in talking to her friends that even that decision had complications. An illegal abortion could cost several hundred dollars or more. She could always find someone willing to do the job for $50 to $100, but she wanted someone she could trust, someone she could be sure would perform the task competently.

As the weeks passed, McCorvey could not locate an abortionist she trusted. Finally, a friend suggested to her that she have the child and give it up for adoption. It was not something McCorvey looked forward to doing, but at the time it seemed to be her best—if not her only—option. She returned to her physician and asked once again for his help. This time, he suggested that she contact a young lawyer who had arranged several private adoptions in the past. The adoptions were handled with the greatest discretion, the doctor assured her, and in the end everyone would be happy. McCorvey eventually agreed to meet with the lawyer.

When the two finally met, McCorvey told him how she had been trying for weeks to obtain an abortion, with no success. The lawyer listened carefully, asked her several more questions, and then suggested she meet with another lawyer, someone who might better be able to serve her needs. This was how McCorvey met Linda Coffee.

Convincing McCorvey to Sue

After McCorvey had finished relaying her story to the two lawyers, Weddington, who had been listening intently, spoke up. She and Coffee had been looking for a woman to be a plaintiff, the complaining party, in an abortion suit, she said. Many people in Texas wanted to change the state's strict abortion laws. Out of nearly a million and a half abortions performed in the United States each year, fewer than ten thousand were done legally.[4] Those women who had illegal abortions ran the risk of experiencing serious medical complications and of being legally prosecuted. Many women risked their very lives at the hands of unscrupulous illegal abortionists.

Then Weddington asked McCorvey how she had felt when she realized she would be unable to have an abortion.

McCorvey replied that she had been angry at being forced by a legal system to have a child that she neither wanted nor felt she could adequately care for. Weddington told her that the system made Coffee and her angry, too, especially in light of studies that showed that legalized abortion was the best solution to several unsafe alternatives.[5] That is why they wanted McCorvey to sue the state to change its laws. Because McCorvey would be the person filing the suit, she would be the plaintiff and possibly have to testify on her own behalf. Weddington assured her, however, that the two lawyers would do most of the talking in court.

After they had presented their case in court, Weddington explained, a judge would decide whether or not McCorvey would be allowed to have an abortion. If he agreed, a precedent would be set for other Texas women in similar situations. In effect, the decision would change Texas abortion laws forever.

It would not be an easy case, Weddington warned. The judge might decide in favor of the plaintiff, striking down the existing Texas laws. But on the other hand, he might decide to strike down only part of the laws or—of course—none of them, thus blocking McCorvey's attempt to obtain a legal abortion. If that happened, it would be unlikely that another woman would ever be able to sue the state to change its laws.

Weddington told McCorvey that she should take some time to think the matter over. The three women left the restaurant together, with Weddington and Coffee feeling that they just might have found the ideal plaintiff for their case. McCorvey, who had already made up her mind, was sure of it.[6]

CHAPTER 2

The "Normalization" of Abortion

T he days passed, one melting into another, until McCorvey heard once more from Coffee and Weddington. The attorneys asked for another meeting to see what they could do to help. They talked about Norma McCorvey, the helpless victim of a vicious rape, and the suit they hoped to bring in her name against the state of Texas.

For a suit, the timing seemed right. In 1969, people were beginning to talk more openly about abortions and a woman's right to pursue them. Opinion polls taken over the previous few years showed that a growing number of women favored changes in state abortion laws, changes that would make it easier for *all* women to obtain abortions. Even among Roman Catholics, the percentage of people generally disapproving of abortion had dropped from 36 in 1962 to 20 percent in 1969.[1]

Challenges for the Case

Not everyone wanted the laws changed, of course. Anti-abortion forces in Texas and elsewhere remained strong. If Coffee and Weddington hoped to win despite the opposition, they would need to present a solid—in fact, a nearly perfect—case. If they failed to do so and the court ruled that the Texas laws were legal, women throughout the state would be forced to endure the consequences for years to come.

That was only one of the problems with which the two lawyers struggled. There were others. Court cases, the lawyers realized, moved maddeningly slowly. Yet it was apparent to Coffee from the start that McCorvey's pregnancy was well into the first, and perhaps as far along as the second, trimester, or three-month period of her nine months of pregnancy. If she were to receive an abortion, she would have to do so quickly, preferably within a matter of weeks. Having an abortion after the first three months would very likely jeopardize the operation and place the mother at increased risk.

Also, there was a growing feeling within the courts that a fetus within its first trimester of development was not yet a fully functioning human being, whereas a fetus in its second trimester *could* be considered a functioning human being—and certainly was in its *third* trimester. The act of allowing a fully developed human being to be aborted during the last two trimesters—those critical six months prior to birth—struck many anti-abortionists, or pro-life advocates, as murder.

With McCorvey so far along, the lawyers realized that there was next to no chance to pursue their suit in time to abort the fetus during the first trimester, and possibly not even by the end of the pregnancy. There was, however, an outside chance they could get the court to agree to issue a temporary restraining order.

A temporary restraining order, or TRO, would allow all Texas women to receive abortions at least until the full case was heard, although it was unlikely that a judge could be persuaded to issue such an order, considering the important nature of the question yet to be decided. Even if they did get a TRO, McCorvey might still have difficulty finding a qualified physician willing to perform the abortion when the question of legalized abortion was still to be ruled upon by the courts. Without a TRO, the best Texas women could hope for was that McCorvey would go ahead with her suit, even though she might be forced in the meantime to have the child.

A Rocky Past

Over the weeks that followed, the lawyers discovered yet another problem with the case. They had gradually become aware from the story that McCorvey had laid out for them that her past had been less than flawless. She had grown up in an unstable family environment. Her father, a military officer, was transferred from one city to another every two or three years, taking his family with him. As a result, McCorvey never stayed in one spot very long and never developed a strong family bond. She had few friends, and even her relationship with her one younger brother was frequently strained. Once, during an interview, she admitted that her brother, whom she called "Punko," was in constant trouble with the authorities. McCorvey thought little better of herself and sometimes referred to herself as "Freako."[2]

By the time her father had left the military and taken a job as an electrician in Dallas, McCorvey's parents were fighting constantly. Her father's heavy drinking aggravated the problem, and McCorvey dreaded going home to the bickering and confusion.[3] She also had her own problems in school—problems that grew worse once her parents finally separated. She eventually dropped out of school in the tenth grade and began work as a waitress at a local drive-in restaurant. Before long, she met and began dating a twenty-year-old drifter, four years her senior, who had dreams of becoming a rock star. The two were soon married and moved to Los Angeles.

McCorvey's problems grew worse when her husband was unable to find work. Then McCorvey became pregnant. When she broke the news to her husband, he yelled at her, called her obscene names, and beat her. That night, after he had fallen asleep, she gathered her belongings and hopped on a bus back to Dallas.

Unfortunately, life back home was little better than it had been in Los Angeles. Once the baby was born, McCorvey tried returning to high school, but she felt out of place, awkward, "like a pool cue in a china cabinet, like a big idiot."[4] To make matters worse, her relationship with her mother, which had never been good, steadily worsened. The two women fought constantly over McCorvey's baby daughter. One night McCorvey was awakened and, while still half asleep, persuaded to sign a legal document that gave her mother custody of the infant. Not long after,

McCorvey's mother and new stepfather moved with the infant to Arkansas, leaving McCorvey in Dallas, alone and penniless.

An Unsympathetic Plaintiff

Coffee and Weddington tried to figure out how to handle these problems as they slowly began to doubt how sympathetic a plaintiff McCorvey would make. What if the court decided to look into her past? How would McCorvey hold up beneath the scrutiny—this woman who had dropped out of high school, gotten married to a drifter at the age of sixteen, had a daughter whom she had given up to her mother, joined a carnival, and in general screwed up her entire life.

And that was not all. From the start, Coffee had been skeptical about McCorvey's tale of rape. Inconsistencies often occur in the stories told by rape victims, but the facts surrounding McCorvey's story were anything but consistent. At first she told Coffee that she had been raped by one man. Later she changed her story, claiming that she had been gang-raped, sometimes insisting that the rapists consisted of several men and McCorvey's two female roommates, while at other times recalling that the rapists were actually three men—one white, one black, and one Hispanic. This last story was particularly hard for Coffee to believe, since it was highly unlikely that three men from such diverse racial backgrounds would have been walking together down a small-town country road in Georgia in 1969.

Yet, in McCorvey's favor, the circumstances behind her pregnancy were not the main question here, and Coffee and

Weddington were determined not to let them become a central part of their suit. With that decided, they next had to determine the best way to keep the rape issue out of the case. This could best be done by not bringing up the subject of rape during the proceedings. The lawyers would need to impress on McCorvey how important this issue was and somehow keep her as far away from a curious press as possible. It simply would not do to have a series of newspaper articles bringing up the rape question halfway through the trial.

These were just some of the concerns racing through the minds of Coffee and Weddington when they next met with McCorvey. They told the pregnant woman that, if she agreed to become plaintiff in the case, she would almost certainly have to bear her child, since it would be virtually impossible for a court to decide her case in time for her to get an abortion.

McCorvey did not hesitate. Yes, she would agree to have the child. At the time, she was four months pregnant, and she knew she would be unlikely to find anyone willing to perform an abortion anyway. The only thing she asked was that her name be kept secret. Although she had had a poor family life, she was still concerned about what her parents might think if they discovered their daughter was having an abortion. McCorvey's father was a Jehovah's Witness and her mother was a Roman Catholic. Both religions staunchly disapprove of abortion, and McCorvey did not want to alienate either of her parents any more than she already had.

Abortion was a controversial issue in the time of the *Roe v. Wade* case, and continues to be a subject for debate today.

Coffee winced. That was the one sticking point she and Weddington had not yet been able to resolve—the publicity likely to surround the case. Abortion had recently become a "hot" moral question in the United States. Hardly a month went by without a women's magazine running an article on the pros and cons of legalized abortion. Almost every day some American newspaper featured an article or a series or an editorial on the subject. Once the press learned about the suit, which would surely happen because of open court records, reporters would begin a relentless search to find the names, dates, and places involved. In short, McCorvey's right to privacy was sure to be jeopardized.

McCorvey saw her dream slowly slipping away. She had already decided that acting as plaintiff in the suit was one of the best things she could do. If she won, her victory would open the doors for thousands upon thousands of women seeking the right to have an abortion. No longer would women have to suffer the agony and trauma, the fears and humiliation that McCorvey had suffered since learning of her pregnancy. By opening the doors to abortion reform, she could finally do something positive with her life—something good and decent. Now, at the last moment, it seemed that the price she might have to pay by surrendering her anonymity might simply be too great.

McCorvey Becomes Jane Roe

Suddenly Weddington had an idea. Why not have McCorvey take on a pseudonym, a false name, to protect her identity?

In that way, the court would have no record of her past, and the press—no matter how hard it dug—would be unlikely to turn up anything beyond what McCorvey herself revealed in court.

McCorvey agreed. A pseudonym would provide her with the greatest amount of protection possible. The three soon settled on the name, Jane Roe.

Coffee and Weddington were nearly convinced that the suit should be filed. They believed they now had a solid case to build against the state's abortion laws, and they felt that most, if not all, of their concerns about McCorvey's past could be handled satisfactorily.[5]

Still, one thing bothered the two attorneys. Could McCorvey guarantee to stick out the suit until the very end? Coffee and Weddington couldn't bear the thought of working for months or even years on a case only to have the plaintiff decide to pull out before the case reached court. To their relief, McCorvey promised to see the suit through to the end, no matter how long it took. She seemed to have developed a keen understanding of the importance of the suit, not only for herself, but also for future generations. Coffee and Weddington were satisfied. Now all that remained was to begin the difficult task of building a solid case. It would not be easy to overturn a Texas state law that had been on the books for more than a century. But, with hard work and the proper preparation, the two lawyers believed that it could be done.

And so did Jane Roe.

CHAPTER 3

A Case for "Jane Roe"

Nearly two months had passed since the initial meeting with Coffee, Weddington, and McCorvey. In particular, McCorvey had spent many days, weeks, and months thinking about the advantages of being able to get an abortion to resolve an unwanted pregnancy. Not for *her* any longer, but for other women who found themselves in similar situations … and then it became time to file the case.

The attorneys decided to challenge five of the six separate articles of the Texas state abortion law—Articles 1191 through 1194 and 1196. These articles prohibited anyone from attempting to obtain or perform an abortion resulting in the destruction or removal of the fetus or embryo from a woman's womb. In addition, the law stated that any abortion attempt resulting in the death of the mother would be considered murder.

Sarah Weddington, one of the main attorneys in the *Roe v. Wade* case, went on to serve three terms in the Texas House of Representatives and served as Special Assistant for Women's Affairs for Jimmy Carter.

The penalty for an abortionist violating these laws ranged from two to five years' imprisonment and a fine of up to one thousand dollars. The only exception was in the case of an abortion by a medical doctor for the sole purpose of saving the life of the mother. Despite the law, countless Texas women sought out illegal abortions each and every year. Some were successful; others were not.

A Personal Connection

Sarah Weddington knew all too well the dangers of obtaining an illegal abortion. She had learned of them as a graduate student in 1967. She was in her third year of law school, dating a man, Ron Weddington, who was in the process of finishing his undergraduate degree after serving in the army. He, too, hoped to attend law school.

Weddington had decided not to have relations with Ron until they began talking of marriage, then she decided it would be safe to enter into relations with him. Several weeks later, she began to worry.

For days, she had run between classes to the women's room of the law school. She hoped that she was wrong, but each day she grew more convinced that it was true. She was pregnant. The questions began to pour through her mind. How would she handle pregnancy and law school at the same time? How would she find time to work between classes? What if she and Ron decided not to get married after all?

Weddington had heard stories of women who had obtained illegal abortions, and they were horrifying. Still, what other options were there? And if she decided to have an abortion, where would she go? Back in the sixties, the newspapers were not exactly filled with such information, and asking around was both impractical and imprudent.

Luckily, her fiancé had heard about a doctor in Piedras Negras, a small Mexican town across the border from Eagle Pass, Texas. The doctor there had had some medical experience in the United States, and he did abortions. Although abortions were illegal in Mexico, too, they were nonetheless widely performed there. Ron called for an appointment, made the arrangements, and planned the trip south.

"I was one of the lucky ones," Weddington said. "The doctor was pleasant and seemed competent; this made me feel more at ease about being there."[1] The doctor explained the abortion procedures to Weddington before finally beginning the task. Luckily, the abortion was successful, and after a few days of rest, the young couple drove back across the border to the United States, but the memories of that dramatic incident remained with them.[2]

Memories of her ordeal visited Weddington often as she and Coffee dug into the exhaustive task of researching their case, scanning various computer data banks for precedent-setting or prior abortion cases. The lawyers planned to base their constitutional challenge to the state's abortion laws on the US Constitution's Fourteenth Amendment, which guaranteed equal protection for everyone under the law, but after several weeks of research, they were disappointed to find few such cases in the law books.

Griswold v. Connecticut

Finally, they discovered an interesting case, *Griswold v. Connecticut*, that could be of value to them.[3] The 1961 Supreme Court case pitted Estelle Griswold, the executive director of the Planned Parenthood League of Connecticut, and Charles Lee Buxton, a respected local physician and head of obstetrics and gynecology at Yale University, against the state of Connecticut. Griswold and Buxton had been arrested for giving birth control information and instructions to a married couple. They were tried in a local court, found guilty, and fined $100 each. They appealed the decision to the Supreme Court.

The counsel for Griswold and Buxton was Fowler Harper, a Yale University law professor and highly regarded First Amendment expert. Harper felt that preventing a doctor from discussing birth control measures with his patients was a violation of free speech, which is protected by the First Amendment.[4] During his research, Harper came across a law journal article by New York University law professor Norman D. Redlich. The article was entitled, "Are There 'Certain Rights' ... Retained by the People?"[5] In it, Redlich argued that, although the right to privacy is never specifically mentioned within the US Constitution, the Ninth Amendment implies its existence. Harper decided to base his case on this right to privacy. He expanded his argument to include all amendments in which the right to privacy was implied, including the First, Third, Fourth, Fifth, Ninth, and Fourteenth.

Finally, in a 1965 decision, noted Supreme Court Justice William O. Douglas wrote the *Griswold* opinion, affirming the right to privacy and striking down the Connecticut statute prohibiting the use of birth control. Douglas found that the Connecticut law, among other things, violated the "zone of privacy" created by several fundamental constitutional guarantees.

In a concurring opinion, Justice Arthur Goldberg, Chief Justice Earl Warren, and Justice William Brennan cited former Justice Louis Brandeis's analysis of the principles underlying the Constitution's guarantees of privacy—aspects of family life in which the government could not meddle.

> The makers of our Constitution undertook to secure conditions favorable to the pursuit of happiness. They recognized the significance of man's spiritual nature, of his feelings and of his intellect. They knew that only a part of the pain, pleasure and satisfactions of life are to be found in material things. They sought to protect Americans in their beliefs, their thoughts, their emotions and their sensations. They [debated] … the right to be let alone—the most comprehensive of rights and the right most valued by civilized men.[6]

In writing his opinion in *Griswold*, Justice Douglas stated clearly that the "right of privacy" was far greater than the words written in the Constitution and included rights not specifically spelled out. He went on to point out that one of the requirements of a free society is freedom from intrusion by the government in home, family, and marital relations.[7]

Coffee and Weddington were elated. If the Supreme Court could uphold the right to privacy for a case involving

Estelle Griswold (L) and Cornelia Jahncke, President of Parenthood League
of Connecticut, Inc., celebrate as they read the court's decision stating the birth
control law is unconstitutional.

birth control, why not for abortion? The two lawyers realized
that it was no sure thing. They knew that the concept of
constitutional privacy was one of the most hotly debated of all
constitutional issues. They also realized that convincing a court
to consider such a new idea as the privacy issue could be difficult.
Still, they decided to base their own case on this concept, since
they had no better viable option.[8]

Making a Case

Once they had made up their minds, the actual preparation for the case went rather quickly. Their argument would be fairly simple: A woman is guaranteed the right to an abortion by her constitutional right to privacy. No state could interfere with a woman's decision to have an abortion, which was a private matter.

The lawyers decided to back up their case with the First Amendment, which includes protection for a person's right to associate with whomever he or she wishes. The Texas abortion law, the two would argue, interfered with a woman's right to associate with her physician.

They also planned to argue their case on the Fourth Amendment, which protects citizens from unreasonable search and seizure. While writing the *Griswold* opinion, Justice Douglas questioned the extent to which the state of Connecticut would need to go in order to enforce its anti-contraception laws, asking, "Would we allow the police to search the sacred precincts of marital bedrooms for telltale signs of the use of contraceptives?"[9]

Coffee and Weddington decided that the Texas laws prohibiting abortions were difficult to enforce and could involve police invasion of a physician's office. Their decision to rely on the Fifth Amendment, which protects a person from self-incrimination, was also based upon Douglas' *Griswold* ruling, which protects the individual by creating a zone of privacy around citizens, safeguarding them from interference by the government.

Then the lawyers decided to include the Eighth Amendment, which forbids cruel and unusual punishment. It was unlikely that a judge would consider that denying a woman the right to an abortion was cruel and unusual punishment, but the attorneys added the argument anyway.

Using the Ninth Amendment was a bit chancy, but they eventually decided to include it in their argument, because it offers strong legal grounds for recognizing a person's right to privacy.

The amendment that seemed to offer the greatest hope, however, was the Fourteenth. It guaranteed everyone equal protection under the law, thus fitting the lawyers' arguments perfectly by prohibiting vaguely written laws and laws that create confusion about who is protected and under what circumstances. The Texas abortion laws were vague, the lawyers would argue, because they created confusion among physicians about what constituted a life-threatening condition. The Texas laws included no clear guidelines and therefore could be unevenly applied. Some Texas physicians interpreted the laws to the letter, performing abortions only when the mother's physical life was threatened. Others interpreted the laws as meaning that abortions could be performed when a woman's mental or physical health was at risk, even though actual death might not occur if the pregnancy were allowed to continue.

At first, Coffee was concerned that relying on the Fourteenth Amendment might take control of a woman's right to have an abortion out of her own hands and place it in the hands of her physician. After all, the court might argue, who is more qualified to determine a woman's mental or physical health than her own doctor? Still, the amendment was a strong argument for the right to privacy, and Weddington convinced Coffee to use it, although both lawyers decided they would concentrate on those amendments that stressed that making the decision to have an abortion was a woman's right.

Deciding on Where to Try the Case

Once their approach to the case was resolved, the question of where the case should be tried came up. Their best chance for success lay in a three-judge federal court. Such courts are geared to hearing suits designed to challenge the constitutionality of various state laws. Three-judge courts also provide a direct appeals route to the US Supreme Court—something that would prove invaluable to the case should the lower court rule in favor of the Texas laws.

Another advantage of presenting the case to a three-judge court was that such courts are obligated to hear a case as soon as the court is convened. That meant that the case would be heard while McCorvey was still pregnant. The lawyers decided to include in their suit an additional case, involving plaintiffs John and Mary Doe (real people using fictitious names), a young couple who had volunteered their services in an abortion suit several months before. Finally, on Tuesday, March 3, 1970, Coffee gathered up all the legal pleadings she had prepared and took them to the federal courthouse to file two separate suits, *Roe v. Wade* and *Does v. Wade*. Both of the suits asked that the Texas abortion statutes or laws be ruled unconstitutional and that the court issue an injunction that would prohibit Henry Wade, the chief law enforcement officer of Dallas County, from enforcing them. The suits claimed that the Texas statutes were unconstitutional because they were vague and violated the plaintiffs' rights to privacy under the First, Fourth, Fifth, Eighth, Ninth, and Fourteenth Amendments.

Word of the suits spread quickly throughout the state. On March 6, the *Dallas Times Herald* published an editorial opposing them. Although the paper admitted that the state's abortion laws were "badly in need of intelligent overhaul," it was far from siding with the plaintiffs, declaring, "We have no sympathy with the attempt of a married couple [the Does] and a single woman to get the existing abortion law declared unconstitutional by a Dallas federal court." Within hours, news stories about the suits broke nationwide. The controversy had begun.

CHAPTER 4
A Case for Henry Wade

I n Dallas, Texas District Attorney Henry Wade was officially served papers notifying him that he was being sued by Jane Roe and John and Mary Doe on March 16, 1970. For the district attorney of *any* state to receive papers was hardly unusual: it happened every day, but in this case in particular, the papers caught Wade's eye.

Wade, who had been district attorney of Dallas County for twenty years, was a highly regarded criminal lawyer who would have prosecuted Lee Harvey Oswald, the assassin of President John F. Kennedy, and who did prosecute Jack Ruby, the man who had killed Oswald before the assassin could be brought to trial. Wade had demonstrated many times in the past his firm belief in maintaining Texas' abortion laws and society's status quo in regard to abortion.[1]

Wade appointed one of his most competent lawyers, John Tolle, to defend against the suit. Tolle, a Roman Catholic who would later become a federal judge in Dallas, had been an undergraduate at the University of Notre Dame before enrolling in Southern Methodist

University Law School. He, like Wade, had spoken both in and outside the courtroom on behalf of the sanctity of the human fetus. In preparing his defense, Tolle reviewed all the medical literature on abortion that he could find. He discovered no surprises, certainly nothing that made him think that an attack on the abortion laws of Texas would be successful. The fetus, according to nearly all of Tolle's medical sources, was a totally separate entity—a distinct human being—from the woman who bore it. What better argument for the right to life was there than that?

Tolle's defense would eventually center on the argument that the fetus had just as much right to life as the mother. He never stopped to think that a court might find the concept that a woman's right to an abortion might outweigh the rights of the fetus to life. To Tolle, the case was clear; the suit was little more than a frivolous waste of taxpayers' money.

Within two days, the Fifth Circuit Court of Appeals named the three justices who would hear *Roe v. Wade* and *Does v. Wade*, the two suits being brought against the state. In order to save both time and money, the court decided to combine the cases under the umbrella suit of *Roe v. Wade*.

Tolle Responds

On March 23, Tolle responded to the suit against Wade by stating that, to the best knowledge of the district attorney's (D.A.'s) office,

---

Henry Wade served as the district attorney of Dallas County from 1951 to 1987.

none of the facts had been proven. So far as Henry Wade was concerned, Jane Roe—a fictitious name—might not even have been a real person.

Tolle also contended that Roe had no right to sue the state because the Texas abortion statute affected only persons who performed abortions. There were no provisions to penalize the women who sought them. Since only the person who performed an abortion could be prosecuted, it therefore made sense that Jane Roe had suffered no legal injury and thus was not entitled to sue for relief. So far as District Attorney Wade and the state of Texas were concerned, Jane Roe might or might not have been a real person with a real problem, but even if she were, she had no legal recourse.

Finally, Tolle discredited the "vagueness" contention of the plaintiffs by stating that, since the law had been on the books for a century without a serious challenge to its constitutionality, it was obvious that it had been understood well enough by the majority of people who had read it over the years—pregnant women and physicians alike.

An Intervener Is Added

The next day, another party asked to intervene on the abortion case. An intervener is someone who, because of a related interest, seeks to join in a lawsuit after it has been started. If the court agrees to allow the intervention, the intervener in effect becomes an additional plaintiff in the case.

Coffee and Weddington were pleased to learn that the intervener in this case was a licensed physician named

Pro-life groups agreed with Tolle's argument. They believed abortion was the murder of a defenseless human being.

James Hallford. Hallford had recently been charged by Henry Wade with the crime of performing an illegal abortion. When Roy Merrill, one of Hallford's attorneys, heard of the *Roe v. Wade* case, he immediately called Coffee and suggested that the two join forces. After all, Merrill argued, *Roe v. Wade* had two shortcomings. First, Coffee and Weddington had not found anyone from the medical profession to support their case. Second, the two lawyers were representing a plaintiff with no actual grievance in the court's eyes, since having an abortion would not penalize McCorvey but, rather, her abortionist. By teaming up with Hallford, Coffee and Weddington would have a stronger case and a greater chance of overturning the Texas abortion laws—something that would obviously benefit everyone concerned. Coffee and Weddington agreed, and on March 24 the court granted Hallford permission to intervene in *Roe v. Wade*.

A Request for a Deposition

Although some of the players in *Roe v. Wade* were beginning to change, the D.A.'s office remained unconcerned. Tolle was confident that the challenge to the state's abortion laws would be soundly defeated. He still had a strong card to play in the game. On March 27, Tolle filed a request with the court to depose, or interview, Jane Roe. His reasons for wanting to take a deposition from her were twofold. First, he wanted to know something about how far along in her pregnancy she was. If she were close to delivering, she would have little or no chance of winning an abortion case, because she would be too advanced to undergo the risk of an abortion. Second, he wanted to learn something about Jane Roe's background. Perhaps she was not as poor as her attorneys claimed. Perhaps she had a husband. Perhaps she was in a position to support both herself and a new baby. Tolle felt that, if he could learn Jane Roe's identity, the press would be likely to do the rest of his work for him, unearthing useful information that Tolle himself might have difficulty uncovering.[2]

Judge Sarah Hughes considered Tolle's request for a deposition for more than a week. Meanwhile, Coffee and

Weddington were beginning to worry. What if the judge decided to grant Tolle his request? Rather than go through the humiliation of revealing embarrassing facts about her past, McCorvey might simply decide to drop the suit, and that, in light of the work the two lawyers had already done, would be a disaster. Slowly but surely, Coffee and Weddington were beginning to see *Roe v. Wade*, the case that a few weeks ago had looked so sound, slip through their fingers.

When Coffee approached McCorvey with the latest turn of events, though, she was relieved to learn that the young woman was determined to go through with the case—even if she had to give Tolle a deposition.

Luckily for the plaintiffs, Judge Hughes decided to rule against Tolle's request for a deposition—with one stipulation. In order to ensure that the facts in the case were accurate as presented, she required that Jane Roe testify under oath, which she did. McCorvey and Coffee then submitted the facts about Jane Roe to the court.

While the following facts came out during the closed testimony, Coffee and Weddington were successful in concealing McCorvey's true identity, along with any information about the circumstances leading to her pregnancy. They had succeeded in keeping McCorvey's past out of the press and away from her parent's watchful eyes. Now they would just have to wait and see what the court would do with the facts that it received. Would concealing Jane Roe's true identity and "questionable" past be successful with the court? Only time would tell.

Juggling for Advantage

Once the affidavit, or sworn written statement, had been taken, the lawyers on both sides began juggling for legal positioning. Tolle asked for a jury trial, which was virtually unheard of in a three-judge court, while Coffee asked that the case be decided on the basis of the facts without hearing additional evidence or having to call witnesses. Keeping McCorvey out of court would ensure that the woman would not accidentally let slip some information that could prove damaging to the case.

In the end, the request for a jury trial was denied, and McCorvey would not be required to testify. The attorneys for both sides filed their briefs, a few pages each of straightforward factual material, and on May 23, Coffee and Weddington appeared before the Fifth Circuit Court of Dallas in order to present their oral arguments. It was Weddington's first courtroom appearance ever, and it was certainly the most important case of Coffee's career.

Judge Hughes' courtroom that morning was filled with spectators, mostly women and reporters. Outside, five pro-choice women carried signs saying, "My body, my decision" and "Compulsory pregnancy is cruel and unusual punishment." Even though the plaintiffs were not required to be present, John and Mary Doe were there; Norma McCorvey, now eight months pregnant, was not. Realizing that opponents of abortion might be demonstrating at the entrance to the court building, she decided to avoid a confrontation.[3]

Even if her lawyers had wanted her there, it was unlikely that McCorvey would have shown up. It often took three or four days for them to get in touch with her, since McCorvey was still moving around from one place to another and was difficult to track down.

In the Fifth Circuit Court, Coffee and Weddington were fortunate to have three highly respected judges. At that time (until *Roe v. Wade*), the court had been best known for its *Brown v. Board of Education* decision, ordering the desegregation of American public schools. The three judges, all Dallasites, were considered by their peers to be among the most learned, experienced, and fair in the nation.[4] The first, William McLaughlin Taylor, had been appointed to the federal bench in 1966 by President Lyndon B. Johnson. Taylor had been a noted trial lawyer before going on the bench. The second, Sarah Tilghman Hughes, was appointed to the federal bench by President John F. Kennedy in 1961 and gained national recognition when she swore in Lyndon Johnson following Kennedy's assassination. The third, the liberal Irving S. Goldberg, another Johnson appointee, was generally admired for his quick wit and courtroom experience. He was also a recipient of the prestigious Brotherhood Citation of the National Conference of Christians and Jews.

As the hearing unfolded, it became obvious that all three justices took the matter far more seriously than did Tolle and the Dallas County D.A.'s office.[5] At one point, Judge Goldberg asked Coffee if she felt that injunctive relief—ordering the state of Texas to stop enforcing its abortion laws—could be required better under the Ninth Amendment than under the First. Coffee jumped at the opening.

I don't think it makes any difference in our case, because whether you say that the rights involved are First Amendment rights or Ninth Amendment rights, I feel they are so important that they deserve the special protection that has been accorded to First Amendment rights. In other words, they involve fundamental human freedoms, which I think recent cases have indicated are beginning to be given the same priority treatment that First Amendment rights have always been afforded.[6]

Once the plaintiffs completed their argument, it was time for the D.A.'s office, which was responsible for defending any challenge to the constitutionality of a state law, to present its argument. The attorney general of Texas, Crawford Martin, chose his assistant attorney general, Robert Flowers, to head the defense. Flowers selected Jay Floyd, his assistant chief, to defend the Texas laws. The state had decided to argue that destroying a fetus in the womb was murder, no different from the act of strangling a three-month-old baby.

Arguments for the Defense

Floyd began the arguments for the defense by stating that the federal court had no reason to hear the case, since none of the plaintiffs had any real basis for the suit. Jane Roe, he argued, had by now either had her baby or was too far pregnant to

Sarah Tilghman Hughes was widely recognized as a staunch supporter of women's rights.

have an abortion. Mary Doe had no right to sue because she was not pregnant.

Tolle continued the defense:

> I believe that we're talking about rights. I think that the most persuasive right that the plaintiffs urge ... is the right to privacy, for want of a better term, and there you get to the point where the state has to regulate conflicting rights—whether the state has got an interest in the life of the unborn child sufficient to regulate the woman's right to privacy. This is a very difficult question, and I think that it is properly a legislative question.
>
> I don't think the state has to have a law at all regulating abortion. I believe the field is such that it can regulate it constitutionally. I personally think, and I think the state's position will be and is, that the right of the child to life is superior to that woman's right to privacy.[7]

It was a solid argument, asserting that the state had to balance two rights—that of the fetus to survive versus that of the mother to privacy. In a way, all liberties are obtained through balance. Protecting the rights of someone accused of committing a crime is often balanced at the expense of the victim. Protecting the rights of a minority member is often balanced at the expense of the majority. Tolle went on to imply that many women sought abortions out of convenience and that their decisions were sometimes made frivolously or lightly.

Tolle's argument carried with it a strong emotional appeal, not only in the courtroom, but also among millions of anti-abortionists across the country. Coffee and Weddington were afraid that his argument had damaged their case. Since his was the last argument to be heard by the court, the two women would have no opportunity to discredit it.

If that were not bad enough, Justice Goldberg then decided to ask one last question. What, he wanted to know, would happen if the court issued an injunction against Henry Wade only? Would every other district attorney in the state be free to continue enforcing Texas' anti-abortion law? After all, the plaintiffs' suit mentioned only Henry Wade, not the entire state of Texas.

Tolle, sensing an opportunity to score points for the defense, jumped up and said, "If the court please, I believe we can cite [an] example. In the *Buchanan* case [a court case of the same year which brought into question the state of Texas' sodomy laws], the court's injunction ran against Henry Wade only, and I don't think it binds anyone else."[8]

Goldberg, clearly concerned, turned to Weddington. "Do you have any response to that?" he asked.

Weddington looked up somewhat sheepishly as she suddenly realized that she and Coffee had made a mistake by limiting the suit only to Henry Wade. "We goofed," she responded.

Indeed they had.

CHAPTER 5
To the Supreme Court

S o, on June 17, 1970, the Fifth Circuit Court, seated in New Orleans, Louisiana, issued its decision. It was only one of thousands it had issued in the past. In fact, the Fifth Circuit Court was one of the busiest in the nation. Issuing decisions to them was like eating or breathing.

Unlike the case with Supreme Court decisions, which are surrounded by a great deal of fanfare, the decision in *Roe v. Wade* drew little attention. A court transcriber typed out the findings and mailed copies of the decision to the lawyers on the case. Three other copies were placed in the mailboxes of two newspaper wire-service organizations and the *New Orleans Times-Picayune*.

The court's decision was only thirteen pages long. It stated in part that the Dallas D.A.'s contention that the plaintiffs had no right to sue was wrong. Jane Roe and Dr. Hallford did indeed have a right to sue, the court had found, although Mary and John Doe did not, since Mary Doe was not involved in a pregnancy and had not suffered injury.

So far as the specific merits of the case were concerned, the court found that the Texas abortion laws were unconstitutional and that a woman *did* have a right to an abortion. The decision said in part:

> On the merits, plaintiffs argue as their principal contention that the Texas abortion laws must be declared unconstitutional because they deprive single women and married couples of their right, secured by the Ninth Amendment, to choose whether to have children. We agree.[1]

In addition, the Fifth Circuit Court found the Texas abortion laws to be unconstitutional because they were vague and exceptionally broad.

So far as Dr. Hallford was concerned, the judges considered the Fourteenth Amendment in their findings, ruling that the Texas laws failed "to provide Dr. Hallford and physicians of his class with proper notice of what acts in their daily practice and consultation will subject them to liability."[2] In other words, the court found that the laws failed to clarify when and how a physician might legally perform an abortion in order to save the mother's life.

The decision went on to ask the following questions in support of their conclusion:

> How likely must death be? Must death be certain if the abortion is not performed? Is it enough that a woman could not undergo birth without an ascertainably higher possibility of death than would normally be the case? What

if the woman threatened suicide if the abortion were not performed? How imminent must death be if the abortion is not performed? Is it sufficient if having the child will shorten the life of the woman by a number of years? These questions simply cannot be answered.

The grave uncertainties ... under the related abortion statutes are more than sufficient to render the Texas abortion law unconstitutional under the due process clause of the Fourteenth Amendment.[3]

Declaratory v. Injunctive Relief

Coffee and Weddington were elated, but while the plaintiffs had won a major victory for pro-choice advocates everywhere, they failed to win what they really wanted. The court had stopped short of issuing an injunction to prevent the state of Texas from continuing its crackdown on abortions. Only with such an injunction would women be truly safe in seeking an abortion. The court defended its action by concluding that the state of Texas rarely took action to enforce its abortion laws and that none of the plaintiffs had actually suffered from the laws—either of which circumstances might have been sufficient to have forced the court to step in and issue an injunction.

So in the end, the plaintiffs won declaratory relief: the court declared that the plaintiffs were entitled to relief from the unconstitutional laws, but they failed to obtain injunctive relief, which would have prevented the state from enforcing the laws. Without an injunction against the state, the court's ruling of

unconstitutionality was like a shark with no teeth. It looked ominous, but it was as meek as a lamb.

On the very day that word of the court's findings reached the D.A.'s office, Henry Wade called a press conference. "Apparently," he told the reporters assembled before him, "we're still free to try them [the abortionists], so we'll do just that."[4] The following day, Texas Attorney General Crawford Martin held a press conference in Austin, the state capital, denouncing the court's finding of unconstitutionality. Texas would, he continued, appeal the decision.

The two state officials merely added fuel to an already smoldering fire. The court had declared the Texas laws unconstitutional, but with no provisions to stop Texas from prosecuting abortionists, were the laws really illegal? Could doctors now perform abortions in cases other than to save the mother's life? As law enforcement agencies around the state called the D.A.'s office with their questions, Wade responded by saying that the law was still on the books; the state was appealing the decision of the court; no injunctions against the state had been issued by the federal court; and the D.A.'s office would continue its efforts to prosecute Dr. Hallford for having performed an illegal abortion.

By refusing to change state policy toward abortion, the attorney general and the Dallas district attorney were taking a firm stand. Now it was up to Coffee and Weddington to react.

Aside from arguing the *Roe v. Wade* case, Linda Coffee worked hard to achieve equal employment opportunities for women in Texas.

They would need to take the case to a higher court in the hope of getting an injunction.

At first, they considered going to the Fifth Circuit Appellate Court, or Court of Appeals. This seemed to be the proper place to take their suit. Then they were advised that they could file an appeal directly to the Supreme Court of the United States.[5] They were entitled to this rare opportunity because the three-judge federal court that had heard their case had failed to grant an injunction.

The appellants, those who were appealing the case, were Jane Roe, Dr. James Hallford, and two new litigants anonymously named the Does. Mary Doe, according to court documents, had been denied an abortion by an Atlanta hospital in April 1970. One week later, her legal aid, attorney Tobiane Schwartz, filed suit against Georgia Attorney General Arthur Bolton.[6] After *Doe v. Bolton* was defeated in the US District Court for the Northern District of Georgia, Schwartz and another attorney, Margie Pitts Hames, decided to join in the suit of *Roe v. Wade* as friends of the court. When the Supreme Court announced that it would hear the case, it stated that it had postponed jurisdiction. That meant that the court had not yet determined whether or not the case should previously have been tried in a state court, rather than in a three-judge federal court. If it found that the case should have been tried in a state court, the Supreme Court case would be considered moot and thrown out. If not, the Court would hear the case and rule on it. It would be up to Coffee and Weddington to convince the Court that the case was *not* moot, that the Supreme Court hearing was indeed proper. This they would try to do in their opening briefs at the beginning of their oral argument.

Help and New Doubts

While the lawyers were preparing the case, they received a call from Roy Lucas, an attorney who had heard about *Roe v. Wade* and called to offer his help. Lucas, through his James Madison Law Institute, volunteered both legal resources and funding, things that the relatively inexperienced Coffee and Weddington needed badly. Lucas estimated that taking the case before the Supreme Court would cost as much as $70,000, including fees for research, writing the brief, printing the brief and records from the previous court hearing, and travel costs.

Coffee and Weddington also received an offer of assistance from the New York chapter of the Association for the Study of Abortion, which provided help in maneuvering through the complex Washington legal system surrounding the Supreme Court.

As the hearing drew near, Weddington began to doubt her own ability to argue the case. After all, her only courtroom appearance so far had been in Dallas. She didn't want to argue *Roe* if there was a chance she wouldn't do a good job. She also wondered about whether or not it was advisable for a woman to argue a case before the Supreme Court—a rare occurrence at the time.[7]

To further erode her confidence, Lucas had recently begun pressuring Weddington to allow him to argue the case. He had argued before the Supreme Court before, he said, and was ready, willing, and able to do so again. Wracked with doubt and beginning to resent Lucas' strong-arm techniques, Weddington called on New York Law School Professor Cyril Means for advice. Means had worked with Lucas in the past. Now he offered Weddington one bit of advice. Stand up to him, he said, and "Tell the son-of-a-bitch to go to hell."[8] Weddington decided to take Means' advice and argue the case herself.

An Impressive Venue

When the thirteen-ton bronze Supreme Court doors swung open at 10 a.m. on December 13, 1971, Weddington was already there. She walked into the Supreme Court building and, like most people visiting the court for the first time, was awed by the magnificence of her surroundings. Later, she would recall her impressions about the majesty of the entire courtroom setting. "When you enter at the back, there are the pews where the lay people sit. And they tell you not to chew gum, and not to write, and not to talk, and not to put your arm on the back of the pews. It's just like church."[9]

Weddington took a seat at the appellants' table next to Linda Coffee and Roy Lucas, who, while not arguing the case, was still entitled to sit in support of counsel. At the appellees' table to the right sat Texas Assistant Attorney General Jay Floyd, his superior, Robert Flowers, and Texas Attorney General Crawford Martin. Oddly enough, neither Norma McCorvey, the plaintiff in the original suit, nor Henry Wade, the defendant, was present.

Just as suddenly as Weddington had come in and been seated, the opening salutation began.

The honorable, the chief justice and the associate justices of the Supreme Court of the United States. Oyez, oyez, oyez, all persons having business before the honorable, the Supreme Court of the United States, are admonished to draw near and give their attention, for the Court is now sitting. God save the United States and this honorable court.

With those hallowed words, the same words used to call the Court to order since its founding in 1789, the velvet curtains parted and seven justices—Hugo Black and John Harlan had recently died and had not yet been replaced—emerged to take their seats on the bench. Chief Justice Warren Burger occupied the center seat, while the other justices sat on either side of him in order of descending seniority.

Questioning Begins

As was the custom, Burger began the questioning, asking whether recent court rulings had resolved any of the issues in Weddington's case, to which she responded no. Then Weddington seized a moment of opportunity to talk for quite some time about her beliefs concerning the Constitution and a woman's right to abortion before being interrupted. One of the justices asked where in the Constitution the right to abortion might lie. Weddington, stumbling momentarily, replied that she believed the Ninth and Fourteenth Amendments supported a woman's right to receive an abortion, adding that the suit in the lower court had been brought under the Ninth and Fourteenth Amendments, as well as under a "variety of others."[10]

Justice Byron White interjected sarcastically, "And anything else that might have been appropriate."[11] Weddington, along with the rest of the court, laughed aloud at White's comment, momentarily cutting through the tension that had filled the air, but the young attorney realized that humor would not win her case, and she had to avoid the illusion that she was unsure of herself or of her commitment to her case.

Then, as Justice Potter Stewart began his questions relating to jurisdiction, Justice William Douglas entered the argument, commenting, "So you're really—you're asserting that the pregnant woman has standing." The justice went on to wonder aloud whether or not Dr. Hallford's indictment by the Dallas district attorney's office might have affected the appellants' right to pursue the case before the Supreme Court. Weddington quickly replied that, even if Hallford were found to be an inappropriate party to the suit, that the finding should not affect the original suit brought by Jane Roe and the Does, who were still subject to injury. This response seemed to satisfy Douglas. Now only one question remained.

Does a Fetus Have Rights?

Weddington was asked if a constitutional defense of the rights of a fetus had ever been decided in a Texas court. Weddington, who had done her homework well, cited a case so recent that the Supreme Court hadn't yet had an opportunity to review it.

The US Supreme Court can inspire awe in people entering for the first time.

In *Thompson v. State*, a Texas doctor being sued for abortion contended that the state was not able to prove that the fetus was alive and well at the time of the abortion.

The question illuminated one of the greatest difficulties in deciding an abortion case. In order for abortion to be considered murder, the existence of a body had to be proved. Even when an abortion was the alleged cause of the death of a fetus, who could really say whether the abortion caused the death or whether the fetus had died, say, five minutes before the abortion? In the law, there could be no presumption of death—and certainly not of murder—without proof.

Weddington then cited hundreds of years of legal precedent in which fetuses were presumed not to have rights in such matters as trusts, wills, and estates. In fact, no one had ever become party to such legal documents prior to birth.

In only a few minutes' time, Weddington had successfully argued that, throughout legal precedent, fetuses had no legal rights, while women, including pregnant women seeking abortions, had every right guaranteed under the US Constitution.

Arguments from the Defense

With Weddington's arguments completed, the chief justice motioned to the attorneys for the appellees, and Floyd rose to begin his defense, stating that the case the Supreme Court was hearing should be declared moot. Since Jane Roe was no longer pregnant (having given birth and placed the child up for adoption that summer), she did not have standing. A justice interrupted, "It's a class action [a single suit brought about by a group of people], isn't it?"[12] Floyd admitted that it was (luckily for the appellants, Coffee and Weddington had previously changed their court petitions to that effect). Floyd then went on to state that he didn't believe any woman in Texas had a right to sue for abortion.

He also argued that the case should be returned to the state because Dr. Hallford was involved there in a criminal prosecution. Then Floyd pointed out that the three-judge federal court in Dallas had granted declaratory relief but failed to grant injunctive relief in its findings. In other words, they had acknowledged the decision but had not taken legal steps to implement changes.

One of the justices then asked Floyd if he thought the Fifth Circuit Court was wrong in having granted declaratory relief and if Floyd felt the Texas abortion laws were constitutional.

Floyd hesitated, then at first answered no before changing his answer. Yes, he said finally, adding that in his opinion the declaratory relief had been wrong.

Then another justice commented that Texas does not attempt to punish a woman who performs an abortion on herself. Floyd replied, "That is correct, Your Honor. And the matter has been brought to my attention: Why not punish for murder? Since you are destroying what you—or what has been said to be a human being."[13] Floyd went on to explain that several states found doctors who performed abortions to be guilty of murder, to which one justice replied, "But that's ordinary felony murder, isn't it?"[14] A felony murder is a killing that occurs during the course of committing a serious crime, as when a bank thief accidentally strikes and kills someone with his car while attempting to make his getaway—a lesser crime than premeditated, or preplanned, murder.

Justice Thurgood Marshall then asked Floyd when the state believed that life began. Was it within the first few weeks of pregnancy?

"At any time, Mr. Justice, we make no distinction," came the response.[15]

"You make no distinction whether there's life or not?" Marshall demanded.

"We say there is life from the moment of impregnation."

"And do you have any scientific data to support that?"

"Well, we begin, Mr. Justice, in our brief, with the development of the human embryo, carrying it through to the development of the fetus, from about seven to nine days after conception."

"Well, what about six days?" Marshall inquired.

"We don't know."

"But this [Texas abortion] statute goes all the way back to one hour," Marshall said.

Floyd found himself growing frustrated with a line of questioning with which he was increasingly uncomfortable. "I don't ... Mr. Justice, there are unanswerable questions in this field, I ... "

The observers in the courtroom, sensing the futility of this line of questioning, suddenly broke into laughter, to which Marshall added, "I withdraw the question," and the court was met with still more laughter.[16]

Next, the court asked Floyd if the Texas abortion laws made any distinctions between the manner in which a woman might find herself pregnant, for example, by rape. Floyd replied that, off the record, he understood the state's policy to be that it could stop "whatever has occurred immediately by the proper procedure in the hospital … "[17]

In short, he was saying that a hospital could abort a woman who had been raped, even though doing so was against Texas law.

Within the matter of a few seconds, Floyd had managed to undo any good he might previously have done by admitting that the state of Texas unofficially made exceptions to its own abortion laws.

And then, as suddenly as it had all begun, the case had been heard and the justices filed out of the courtroom. Only one thing remained now—their eventual decision.

On the appellants' side, the arguments were straight forward and forceful.

On the appellees' side, the arguments were somewhat more muddled and unclear.

CHAPTER 6

Return Engagement

W hen the members of the Supreme Court meet in conference to discuss the merits of a case, they do so while following a strict routine. The chief justice speaks first, outlining the most important issues of the case. The other justices follow in order of seniority, each one offering his or her own opinions. No one ever interrupts; everyone talks for as long as he wishes.

That is how the week of December 16, 1971, began, with Chief Justice Burger leading off, but Burger, who often was unprepared for conferences anyway, soon ran into problems. He had difficulty summarizing his thoughts on abortion.[1] A well-known supporter of states' rights, he seemed to favor upholding the Texas abortion laws, although he also implied that he felt the laws were vague and, thus, very likely unconstitutional.[2] Justice White, on the

Justice William O. Douglas served on the US Supreme Court from 1939 to 1975.

other hand, believed strongly that the Texas laws were valid and should not be overturned.[3]

On the other side of the question, Justices Douglas, Marshall, and Brennan believed that a woman had a constitutional right to obtain an abortion. Justices Stewart and Blackmun, on the other hand, favored overturning parts but not all of the Texas laws. The results, then, seemed to be five votes to two in favor of overturning at least some parts of the Texas laws.

Burger wrote in a memo on Monday, December 20, that he felt the voting had been too vague to decide a clear majority, which was necessary to reach a decision.[4] In any event, he wrote that both *Roe v. Wade* and the Georgia case of *Doe v. Bolton* were "quite probably candidates for reargument." The chief justice assigned the task of writing the Court's opinion, or findings, to Justice Blackmun.

A Delayed Opinion

Blackmun did not produce a rough draft of the opinion until the following May. He shared the draft with several other justices, who felt that it was not as well written or thought out as it needed to be.[5] Justice Douglas suggested that Blackmun expand the opinion to include more references to a woman's right to do what she wanted with her own body. He also expressed the feeling that there was really no need to reargue the cases, especially *Doe v. Bolton.*

But something else was bothering Douglas. He had felt from the very beginning that Burger wanted to delay the decision for political reasons, mostly to avoid embarrassing President Richard M. Nixon, who was strongly opposed to abortion.[6] In the meantime, two new Nixon appointees to the Court, Lewis Powell and William Rehnquist, had been approved by Congress. In a conference that June, the two new justices joined in a vote to hold the case over for reargument until the next term.

Douglas, the Court's most liberal justice, was furious. Politics was being dispensed here, he felt, not justice.[7] For a time, he threatened to break one of the Court's oldest unwritten laws by leaking the story of the Court's political squabbling to the press. After several days, though, he was persuaded to drop his dissent, and in 1972, the Court announced that the Texas and Georgia abortion cases were being held over for reargument. When Weddington learned that the Court had decided to reargue the case, she, like most other pro-choice advocates, was bitterly disappointed. She had spent nearly two years of her life working on *Roe v. Wade*. Now it looked as if she would have to spend yet another summer.

Weddington and Coffee joined with Bruner and Merrill, the attorneys for Dr. Hallford, in preparing an additional brief for the reargument. In it, they informed the Court of several new developments in cases involving abortion. The brief concentrated on pointing out a growing national trend toward denying legal rights to the fetus prior to birth. In this way, the attorneys hoped to persuade the Court that a fetus was not a human being until birth and thus an abortion could not be denied to a woman on the grounds that abortion was murder.

Rearguing the Case

Finally, the reargument of the case was set for October 10, 1972. The only unknown factor was the presence on the bench of the two new justices, Rehnquist and Powell. No one was quite sure about their feelings toward abortion; no one could predict how the two would vote.

At the appellants' table sat Weddington, her husband Ron (also an attorney), and Coffee. Opposite them at the appellees' table were Jay Floyd, Robert Flowers (Texas' assistant attorney general, who had taken over from Floyd), and Attorney General Crawford Martin.

The attorney general's office knew that Douglas, Brennan, and Marshall—the three most outspoken justices in favor of reforming the states' abortion laws—would probably vote to strike down the Texas laws, but they were convinced that White could be won over to their side, and they believed from some strong statements Blackmun had made regarding pornography, that the justice was solidly against reforming the Texas laws. In effect, Blackmun was in favor of allowing a state to make laws about its own morality, which in the *Roe v. Wade* case translated into allowing Texas to enact its own abortion laws.

Flowers also speculated that the two new Nixon appointees, Powell and Rehnquist, would, like the man who had nominated them to the Court, be solidly anti-abortion. That would place the *Roe v. Wade* vote at four to three in Texas' favor. Flowers believed he had the case sewn up.

At 10:04 a.m., the reargument of *Roe v. Wade* began. Weddington opened the oral arguments by reminding the Court that Dr. Hallford had joined the case after it had been filed, thus emphasizing that regardless of the Court's findings regarding him, *Roe* took precedence. She also informed the Court that, since the first hearing, more Texas women than ever had begun traveling to New York State to obtain legal abortions.

After several uninterrupted minutes, Justice White asked Weddington a question about whether a state's interest could ever outweigh a constitutional law. "If the State could show that the fetus was a person under the Fourteenth Amendment, or under some other amendment," Weddington replied, "then you would have ... a compelling interest which, in some instances, can outweigh a fundamental right. This is not the case in this particular situation."[8]

Then White asked if Texas differentiated between a pregnant woman in her first month and one in her ninth.

"Our statute does not," she replied, admitting that some states made a distinction about the fetus's development depending upon the length of the pregnancy, but that even those states allowed abortion when the mother's life was threatened and in cases of rape and incest.[9] Finally, White asked, "Well, if it were established that an unborn fetus is a person ... you would have almost an impossible case here, would you not?"

"I would have a very difficult case," she replied, immediately regretting her answer.[10] She had somehow allowed White to back her into a corner on an issue she had not previously considered seriously.

After several other brief questions, Blackmun referred Weddington to a recent Supreme Court decision on capital punishment, asking her if she thought there would be "any inconsistency" in the Court's supporting abortion at the same time that it struck down the death penalty.

Weddington quickly replied that there would be none, since the fetus was not considered a person within the meaning of the Constitution.

"Well, do I get from this, then, that your case depends primarily on the proposition that the fetus has no constitutional rights?" asked Brennan.[11]

Weddington replied, "It depends on saying that the woman has a fundamental constitutional right and that the State has not proved any compelling interest for regulation in the area. Even if the Court at some point determined the fetus to be entitled to constitutional protection, you would still get back into the weighing of one life against another."[12]

Then Stewart, echoing White's earlier question, asked, "Well, if it were established that an unborn fetus is a person within the protection of the Fourteenth Amendment, you would have almost an impossible case here, would you not?"[13]

Weddington had to admit that she would, but she reiterated that the fetus had never before been given legal rights or treated as a living person for legal purposes.[14]

That was the end of Weddington's argument. It had come and gone so quickly that the attorney feared for a moment the Court was simply going through the necessary motions of asking a few questions, and that the justices had already made up their minds about their findings.[15] Still, she could not tell which way they might be leaning. Next, Flowers stood to press his argument.

These were the nine justices sitting on the Supreme Court as of January 1972.
Left to right in the front row is Potter Stewart, William O. Douglas, Chief Justice
Warren E. Burger, Associate Justices William J. Brennan, and Byron R. White.
In the back row is Associate Justices Lewis F. Powell, Thurgood Marshall,
Harry A. Blackmun, and William H. Rehnquist.

He decided to argue two basic concepts. First, abortion was a
state issue and should be decided by the individual states, not the
Supreme Court. Second, it had long been the position of the state
of Texas, he said, that a human being began life upon conception
and was a person within the concept of the Constitution of the
United States, as well as that of Texas.

Justice Stewart interrupted him with a sharp question. "Now how should that question be decided? Is it a legal question, a constitutional question, a medical question, a philosophical question, or a religious question, or what is it?"[16]

Flowers hesitated for several seconds before responding that it could best be decided by the state legislature, which would have the availability of leading medical testimony on which to base their decision.

"So then it's basically a medical question?" Stewart asked.[17]

Fearing for a moment that the Court might decide to throw the case out, Flowers, growing increasingly flustered, backpedaled. "From a constitutional standpoint, no, sir. I think it's fairly and squarely before this Court … "[18]

Stewart then asked if Flowers knew of any case anywhere that held that an unborn fetus was a person within the meaning of the Fourteenth Amendment. Flowers responded that he did not, adding, "We can only go back to what the framers of our Constitution had in mind."[19]

Obviously annoyed by Flowers' lack of knowledge of constitutional law, Stewart proceeded to give the attorney a brief history lesson, reminding him that the Fourteenth Amendment had not been written by the framers of the Constitution, adding "It came along much later."[20]

Stewart then asked if abortion was the only medical surgery to which the state of Texas applied so many restrictions. Flowers said he thought it was. As the justices continued asking him questions he had not anticipated, Flowers' answers grew shorter and his lack of preparation for the case became more obvious.

Even some of his general statements were challenged by the Court. When Flowers alleged that a fetus was very similar to a baby, the Court asked him to produce some medical evidence to support his claim. He responded that he couldn't.[21] Suddenly the assistant attorney general's case was slipping away. He wished, he would later admit, that he had spent more time in preparation.

Following Flowers' poor performance, Weddington was granted a five-minute period for rebuttal. Sensing that she now had the majority of the Court on her side, she stood up and offered a strong reply to Flowers' argument. The Texas abortion laws violated a woman's basic liberty and were therefore unconstitutional, she insisted. The Court had no alternative but to find that women had a constitutional right to abortion.

Weddington concluded her rebuttal and took her seat next to Coffee. The two attorneys watched for some sign that they had won their case as the justices rose and left the room. They knew they had a chance, and after the performance of the Texas attorney general's office, the justices just might be on their side. They hoped and prayed they were right.

Now, as the courtroom slowly began to clear, they knew there was only one sure way to find out. They would simply have to wait. And wait.

And wait.

Associate Justice Blackmun was reported to have said, a year after the ruling on *Roe v. Wade*, that the decision made in the case "will be regarded as one of the worst mistakes in the court's history or one of its greatest decisions, a turning point."

CHAPTER 7

Settling In

J ustice Blackmun had gotten the nod to write the Court's opinion. It wasn't until October 1972 before he completed his first draft and circulated it among the other justices for their input. In response, Justice Brennan wrote a 48-page memo of suggestions, which he sent to Blackmun's chambers for consideration. Blackmun read them carefully and, for the most part, approved. He incorporated them into his opinion.

Then Justice Stewart noted that Blackmun hadn't adequately clarified that a fetus is not a person entitled to personal liberty under the Fourteenth Amendment. So, Blackmun included a section listing numerous constitutional references to legal persons, none of which had ever been used to grant legal rights to a fetus.

Chief Justice Burger also read the opinion and basically opposed it, but Blackmun had anticipated that problem. He decided to incorporate into his opinion a dividing line that broke pregnancy down into three trimesters. These, he felt, could be used as a guideline for limiting a woman's right to abortion. That satisfied Burger.

But incorporating such rigid guidelines now upset Justice Marshall, who objected to limiting the availability of abortions to predetermined "cutoff points." Once again, Blackmun revised his opinion, changing the wording to reflect a more liberal approach to the timing of abortions. One "'compelling point,'" he wrote, "is at approximately the end of the first trimester." By adding the word "approximately," Blackmun had successfully managed to sidestep Marshall's objection.

By early December, the final draft of the revised opinion was ready. Blackmun had recommended striking down the Texas laws. Justices White and Rehnquist had advised the Court that they would dissent. At this point, the vote stood at six to two (with Justices Powell and Douglas siding with Roe). Chief Justice Burger remained undecided.

When the Court met again after the Christmas holidays, the justices were eager to release their decision, but Burger still had not committed himself one way or the other. President Nixon, who was solidly anti-abortion in his sentiments, had won reelection the previous November. It appeared as if Burger did not want to embarrass the president with a pro-abortion decision shortly before the January inauguration.[1]

An Ultimatum and a Decision

Finally, Stewart issued an ultimatum, telling Burger that he should vote one way or the other or allow the Court to render a decision without him. There was no room in the Supreme Court for politics, Stewart pointed out. Burger, a lifelong Republican and an influential political player, did not want to miss an opportunity to cast his vote in the majority, especially in a landmark case such as this, so he finally announced to the Court that he would vote with the majority. That left Rehnquist and White the sole dissenters.

On Monday, January 22, the Supreme Court was filled with anxious people. Although the Court's decision is supposed to remain secret until officially released, somehow the results of the vote, and even the individual opinions of the justices, had been leaked to the press. The entire proceeding was beginning to take on the air of a three-ring circus.

Finally, Blackmun read the Court's opinion:

We forthwith acknowledge our awareness of the sensitive and emotional nature of the abortion controversy, of the vigorous opposing views, even among physicians, and of the deep and seemingly absolute convictions that the subject inspires. One's philosophy, one's experiences, one's exposure to the raw edges of human experience, one's religious training, one's attitudes toward life and family and their values, and the moral standards one establishes and seeks to observe, are all likely to influence and to color one's thinking and conclusions about abortion.[2]

As had been the case in the lower court, the Supreme Court ruled that the Does had no standing to sue, since their case was not based upon a pregnancy and therefore presented no real controversy. Also, since the Court was not anxious to interfere in the affairs of state government any more than absolutely necessary, it threw out the case of Dr. Hallford. Now only the case of Jane Roe remained to be resolved, and since the decision to strike down the Texas abortion laws had already been leaked to the press, all that was left to learn was what limits the Court might place on a woman's right to seek an abortion.

The Court noted that the contention of the state of Texas that the *Roe* case was moot because the mother's pregnancy had ended was incorrect, citing, "The normal 266-day human gestation period is so short that the pregnancy will come to term before the usual appellate process is complete. If that termination makes a case moot, pregnancy litigation will seldom survive much beyond the trial stage, and appellate review will be effectively denied. Our law should not be that rigid … "[3]

The Court went on to state that the right of privacy is broad enough to include a woman's decision to terminate her pregnancy. This right, it said, was based upon the Fourteenth Amendment's concept of personal liberty, as well as the Ninth Amendment's reservation of rights to the people.

Finally, the Court added a restriction to its findings, something it called protecting "potential life." This was a remarkable concept that no one had anticipated. In effect, the Court spelled out exactly how the states could, if they chose to do so, limit a woman's right to abortion. Blackmun stated that the right to abortion changed at various stages of pregnancy. In the first trimester, the state could not intervene in any way to regulate abortion. In the second trimester, it could intervene only to protect a woman's health. In the third trimester, once the fetus "presumably has the capability of meaningful life outside the mother's womb," a period Blackmun called "viability", the state could intervene to protect it.[4]

News of the *Roe v. Wade* decision spread quickly throughout Washington and would have made front-page headlines in every paper in the country except for one curious incident. On the same day that the decision was handed down, former President Lyndon B. Johnson died.

Weddington, at home when the decision was announced, learned of the Court's ruling through a telephone call. "Congratulations," a friend told her. "For what?" Weddington asked. "You won your case," the friend said.[5] Coffee learned of the decision from the radio while driving to work that morning.

Meanwhile, back home in Texas, Norma McCorvey read about the decision in her local newspaper later that night. She immediately burst into tears. A friend who was with her looked at the paper, turned to McCorvey, and asked, "Don't tell me you knew Lyndon Johnson?"

"No," McCorvey replied. "I'm Jane Roe."[6]

When Weddington telephoned McCorvey several days later to ask how she felt, knowing that she had helped to change millions of women's lives for the better, McCorvey replied, "It makes me feel like I'm on top of Mt. Everest."[7]

Across the nation, pro-choice supporters were celebrating. Never in their wildest dreams had they expected to win such a sweeping victory so quickly, but not everyone was pleased with the Court's decision. Anti-abortionists were stunned, and the

Roman Catholic Church, long opposed to abortion under almost any circumstances, was outraged. John Cardinal Krol, president of the National Catholic Conference, indicted the Court for opening the doors to the "greatest slaughter of innocent life in the history of mankind." Texas Archbishop Francis J. Furey labeled the drafters of the decision "fetal muggers." Two conservative Catholic publications demanded the excommunication of Justice Brennan.

That was only the beginning of the controversy. The anti-abortion supporters who had been so confident that the Court would rule in favor of maintaining the Texas laws were left reeling. So, they vowed to join forces and fight the decision in every way possible. The long and grueling war that pro-choice forces believed had finally ended was actually only beginning. In the years to come, the battle would intensify, and a nation that once stood divided over the question of abortion rights would split even further apart.

CHAPTER 8
Settling Down

The Court's decision in *Roe v. Wade* could have helped resolve the nation's angst in addressing the question of the right of a woman to control her own body versus the right of an unborn child to life. It did not.

Following the decision, many Americans were left angered and disillusioned. To most anti-abortionists, the Court had gone too far toward making childbearing more a convenience than a right or a responsibility. It had overstepped its boundaries by creating a new legal right, one that was not in the Constitution and had no real basis for its existence. Nowhere in the document upon which the framework of American law is based is there a mention of the right of privacy. Pro-choice advocates disagreed, of course, as did the Supreme Court justices who had decided the case.

But even many pro-choicers found fault with the Court's ruling, most notably with the concept of viability, or the time at which a fetus is able to sustain life outside the mother's womb.

At the time of *Roe*, most doctors placed viability for an average fetus at around the twenty-seventh week of pregnancy, but advances in medical science had soon pushed the point of viability forward, until today it stands somewhere closer to the twenty-first week. In theory, it is possible that continued advances could push viability still farther forward, perhaps to the sixteenth or even the fifteenth week or earlier. That would shorten the period during which a woman is entitled to seek an abortion under *Roe*. Many pro-choice advocates felt that so hard won a victory should not be eroded because of continuing advances in medical technology.[1]

The Impact of the Decision

Regardless of the consequences of the Court's ruling, the decision took effect immediately, leaving Texas and some thirty other states with no effective legal abortion laws. Since all state and federal courts were bound by the decision, *Roe v. Wade* essentially brought to an end all pending court cases on abortion.

Within weeks of the decision, anti-abortion advocates met to outline their strategy. It included three major goals. First, they would work for the passage of a constitutional amendment declaring fetuses to be legal persons. Such an amendment would in effect invalidate the *Roe v. Wade* decision and reinstate the murder penalty for abortionists. Second, they would pressure state legislatures to pass laws restricting abortion as much as possible, given the frameworks of *Roe*. Third, they would attempt to cut off funding for abortions through pressure placed on state legislatures nationwide.

At the same time, anti-abortionists, who now began calling themselves pro-life supporters, labeled January 22, the date of the Court's decision, "Black Monday," and they determined to march in protest on each anniversary. They began harassing abortion clinics and hospitals, picketing state legislatures, and blocking clinic entrances to women seeking abortions. They placed pressure on physicians not to perform abortions, despite their new legal right to do so, and even attempted to press criminal charges against doctors who performed them.

As was expected, the pro-life fight was led by the Catholic Church. At their annual meeting in the spring of 1973, the US Catholic Conference of Bishops declared their wholehearted support for the overthrow of the *Roe* decision. Mail campaigns were launched. Advertising blitzes were begun. Two years later, the conference unanimously adopted the Pastoral Plan for Pro-Life Activities. This plan provided for the Church's use of its resources to do whatever was necessary to end abortion.

Of all these tactics, the effort to limit government funding for abortions soon proved to be the most successful. By 1980, legislators feeling the impact of public opinion had voted to limit public money for abortion to cases in which the mother's life was at risk, as well as to cases of rape and incest. That same year, the *Christian Science Monitor* reported that the Reverend Jerry Falwell's political organization, the Moral Majority, had begun urging the members of some 72,000 churches nationwide to register to vote in the upcoming presidential election. Their goal:

Here a pro-life activist protesting outside an abortion clinic is carried off by the police.

to elect pro-life candidate Ronald Reagan to the presidency. They were successful.

With Reagan in the White House, pro-lifers received a giant moral boost. The year following Reagan's election, more than 50,000 abortion foes staged a March for Life in Washington, D.C. Representatives of the marchers met with the president and several of his administration officials to form an anti-abortion caucus in Congress. It was aimed at pressuring representatives to enact new legislation. Meanwhile, several states had begun imposing arbitrary roadblocks to women seeking abortions.

Some required a twenty-four-hour waiting period between a woman's signing an abortion consent form and being granted an abortion. Some demanded that second-trimester abortions be performed in hospitals, a far more expensive alternative to clinics.

Finally, the Supreme Court agreed to rule on the constitutionality of these and other obstacles to abortion, and on June 15, 1983, it decided in *Akron v. Akron Center for Reproductive Health* that a state could not impose restrictions on first-trimester abortions and could do so on second-trimester abortions only when there was a "reasonable medical basis" for doing so.[2]

Meanwhile, Reagan increased his anti-abortion rhetoric from the White House. In a letter he sent to various pro-life groups, he stated, "We have waited for ten years for Congress to rectify the tragedy of *Roe v. Wade*. The time for action is now. I assure you that in the 98th Congress I will support any appropriate legislation that will restrict abortion."[3]

As the end of Reagan's first term in office grew near and the 1984 presidential election began, both sides of the abortion debate realized that the incoming president was likely to have a major influence on the makeup of the Supreme Court. Reagan had already appointed to the Court Sandra Day O'Connor, who, true to her political allegiance, had dissented, or stood opposed, in the *Akron* case. Five other justices, all of whom had voted for *Roe*, were more than seventy-five years old. It appeared likely that Brennan, Burger, Powell, Marshall, and Blackmun would soon be replaced. Pro-life supporters wanted Reagan to be able to name their replacements.

Meanwhile, the pro-choice camp was mounting its own campaign. The National Association for the Repeal of Abortion Laws, or NARAL, had made Reagan's defeat its priority. "He is the most staunchly anti-choice president in the country's history," said Executive Director Nanette Falkenberg. "If he is reelected, President Reagan may well have the opportunity to appoint at least two new justices to the Supreme Court ... enough to overturn *Roe v. Wade* and thus make abortions illegal."[4]

The words proved to be at least partly true. In November, Reagan won reelection, and Chief Justice Burger resigned. Reagan named Rehnquist as chief justice, who was now free to use his newfound power and prestige to work against *Roe*. Reagan then appointed Antonin Scalia, a Roman Catholic and pro-life supporter, to occupy the seat vacated when Rehnquist moved up to the position of chief justice. A year later, in 1987, Powell resigned, and Reagan nominee Anthony Kennedy was seated. Although Kennedy had stated he believed in a "zone of liberty, a zone of protection" for individual rights and privacy, Reagan aides who had checked on Kennedy's background prior to his nomination were told that he supported the overthrow of *Roe v. Wade*.

It was now clear that the 7-to-2 majority of Supreme Court justices who had adopted *Roe* was shrinking rapidly with every new Reagan Court appointee.[5] Yet, in an NBC poll taken in October, 1988, some 64 percent of all Americans responding said they wanted to keep legalized abortion.[6] "Many people we deal with have grown up with legal abortions," according to Emily Tynes, a one-time NARAL official. "They feel it's a fundamental right that's part of their world."[7]

But by November 1988, pro-choice backers were destined to lose still more ground with the election of George Bush to the presidency. Just two days after the election, US Attorney General Dick Thornburgh, a firm anti-abortionist, filed a brief asking the Supreme Court to hear a case from Missouri. "If the Court is prepared to reconsider *Roe v. Wade*," he argued, "this case presents an appropriate opportunity for doing so."[8]

The case involved a Missouri law stating that life begins at conception and that no public funds could be used either to perform an abortion or to counsel women about the option. The law specified that no abortion could be performed in a public hospital or facility; that no publicly employed doctor or other personnel could perform or assist in an abortion; and that if a woman was twenty or more weeks pregnant, certain tests for viability (the ability of a fetus to survive outside the womb) were required. Pro-choice forces protested the Missouri law, which in effect reversed the findings of *Roe*. If the Court found the statute constitutional, America would see an increase in the rate of illegitimate births and teenage pregnancies, they argued. Pro-lifers, on the other hand, disagreed, claiming that banning abortion would encourage people to be more careful when having sex. "Once the law tells us that abortion is illegal," said Dr. John Willke, president of the National Right to Life Committee, "there will be far fewer pregnancies to abort."[9]

Finally, on July 3, 1989, the Court issued its decision, upholding each of the specific restrictions in the Missouri bill. Now Missouri, along with any other state wishing to enact similar laws, was free to enforce them. The Supreme Court had failed to overturn *Roe v. Wade*, but it was beginning to move toward returning restrictive abortion rights to the states, where they had resided before *Roe*.

Even More Confusion

Adding even more confusion to the question, Sandra Race Bensing-Cano, the original Mary Doe in *Doe v. Bolton*, came forward in an interview with the *Atlanta Journal-Constitution* and stated that she had been tricked by her attorneys into entering *Roe v. Wade*. "Mary Doe didn't have an abortion. Mary Doe won't ever have an abortion," Bensing-Cano told reporters. "Participating in that case was the biggest mistake I ever made."[10] She went on to claim that her legal aid attorneys had told her "if I agreed to go through the courts [with *Roe v. Wade*], they would not force me to have an abortion."[11]

Adding to their mounting problems, pro-choicers soon lost two more critical legal battles. On June 26, 1990, in *Hodgson v. Minnesota*, the Supreme Court voted five to four to allow individual states to require that a pregnant minor inform both parents before being able to obtain an abortion. Shortly thereafter, the Court, which by then included new Bush appointee David Souter, voted to prohibit employees of government-funded health-and-family-planning clinics from telling pregnant women about abortion. Instead, they were advised to counsel women that abortion was not considered an approved method of family planning.[12]

Bush's final appointee, Clarence Thomas, was confirmed on October 15, 1991. At last, pro-life advocates had in place the support they needed to overturn *Roe v. Wade.* "Since then," said Weddington, "we have simply been waiting for the Supreme Court to observe the final formalities and sign the death certificate."[13] So far, that has not occurred.

Meanwhile, with the 1992 election of Democrat Bill Clinton to the presidency and the unexpectedly early resignation of Justice White, pro-choice advocates saw the first Supreme Court nominee appointed by a Democratic president in sixteen years. Pro-choice forces were further encouraged when Clinton, in one of his earliest political moves following election to office, ordered the lifting of the "Gag Rule" that had for years prevented federally funded abortion clinics from counseling women about abortion. The president also announced a restoration of federal funding for fetal tissue research.

Court-watchers wondered: Would such moves be a case of too little, too late to save *Roe*? Pro-lifers said yes; in their view, it was only a matter of time before the *Roe* decision would be overturned. Pro-choice advocates, on the other hand, could only sit back and wait, hoping there was still time to salvage the landmark Supreme Court decision that began in a small restaurant in Texas so many years ago.

CHAPTER 9
The Making of a Precedent

In more than four decades since its landmark 1973 *Roe v. Wade* decision legalizing abortion, the Supreme Court has weighed in on the abortion issue on numerous occasions. Sometimes it has upheld the availability of abortion granted by *Roe*; more often than not, it has leaned toward restricting that availability.

Regardless, the Court has repeatedly upheld *Roe's* central premise: that the US Constitution guarantees a right of privacy, and that right of privacy includes a woman's right to have an abortion during the first thirteen weeks of pregnancy (and even after that if necessary in order to safeguard the woman's life, health, or well-being).

But along the way, the anti-abortion (pro-life) movement has convinced legislators in Congress to enact a host of laws aimed at reducing *Roe's* effects. Some of these laws require parental notification (in the case of underage females), spousal consent (in the case of married females), or a waiting period before the abortion procedure may be legally performed. Other laws require that women having second-trimester abortions do so in a hospital, rather than in a non-hospital clinic. They also require that physicians use abortion methods that are least harmful to the fetus; that is, they must use methods that will most likely result in the *survival* of the fetus after removing it from the mother's womb. More recent laws and regulations also prevent public funds from tax revenues from being spent on abortion procedures.

The legislative flood of new laws over the years has led to a string of Supreme Court challenges and rulings that have served not only to limit the scope of *Roe*, but also to establish *Roe* as a legal precedent. In so doing, *Roe* has become the "norm" against which all abortion law challenges are measured.

Although there have not been many *critical* Supreme Court rulings on the topic of abortion since the Court's 1973 *Roe* decision, there have been several that are considered important, either to the challenges facing the pro-life groups or those who favor pro-choice (pro-abortion) stands. Here are some of the more recent.

Planned Parenthood of Southeastern Pennsylvania v. Casey

In 1992, in a 5-to-4 vote, the Court upheld all but one provision of Pennsylvania's Abortion Control Act. In the case, *Planned Parenthood of Southeastern Pennsylvania v. Casey*, the Court agreed that Pennsylvania abortion patients in their first trimester

Planned Parenthood provides reproductive health services to patients. Today it serves more than 2.5 million people across the country.

(three months) of pregnancy must receive an "informed consent" booklet to educate them on the abortion process. The Court also agreed that patients could be required to wait twenty-four hours before being granted an abortion. In addition, it recognized that underage (minor) females had to receive written consent from at least one parent. Although the Court had struck down similar provisions in earlier rulings (specifically in the cases *Thornburgh* and *Akron*), it ruled that only restrictions that imposed an "undue burden" on the pregnant woman would be set aside. The Pennsylvania law, it decided, did not.

While upholding the majority of Pennsylvania's Abortion Control Act, the Court refused to acknowledge the requirement that a married woman notify her husband before undergoing an abortion. On that account, the Court's ruling conflicted with that of a lower appellate court judge who had previously found the requirement to be legal. At the time, Supreme Court nominee Samuel Alito of the Third District Court of Appeals wrote that, because the Pennsylvania law included a provision allowing a woman to skip the process of notifying her husband if she believed she might suffer mental or physical abuse from him, the law did not present an "undue burden."

In its 1992 affirmation of *Roe,* the Court found in favor of maintaining the constitutional status quo, supporting the major provisions of *Roe v. Wade,* but, at the same time, the Court also appeared to surpass legal precedent.

"The Constitution serves human values," wrote Justices Kennedy, Souter, and O'Connor, "and while the effect of reliance on *Roe* cannot be exactly measured, neither can the certain costs of overruling *Roe* for people who have ordered their thinking and living around that case be dismissed." In other words, the justices were arguing, *Roe* created expectations that should not be casually ignored or discarded.

At the same time, the Court partially dismantled and modified the trimester framework that *Roe* had created. In doing so, it lightened the legal standard by which laws restricting abortion would be evaluated. Under *Casey*, states were free to regulate abortion during the entire period before fetal viability (the age at which a fetus could potentially live outside the mother's womb, even if only with the use of artificial aid such as oxygen). Furthermore, the states could do so for reasons *other than* to protect the health of the mother.

The joint opinion of the Court also dispensed with the "strict scrutiny" standard of judicial review, which is the toughest and most rigid legal standard by which courts may determine whether or not a law meets constitutional requirements. Since the ruling in *Roe* had declared that access to abortion was a "fundamental right" and that states could regulate it prior to fetal viability only when there was a "compelling state interest," subsequent abortion statutes had been evaluated under strict scrutiny. As a result, in the years immediately following *Roe*, many abortion regulations were declared unconstitutional.

But the Supreme Court in *Casey* replaced "strict scrutiny" with a new and less rigid "undue burden" standard. From that moment on, a pre-viability abortion regulation would be declared unconstitutional *only* if it imposed an undue burden on a woman's right to terminate her pregnancy.

In effect, *Casey* lent support to both sides in the abortion debate. By partly dismantling the trimester system and creating the "undue burden" standard for determining the constitutional right to abortion, the Court gave states greater latitude to regulate abortion in the first five to six months of pregnancy. The Court in *Casey* applied the undue burden standard to the Pennsylvania laws and, with the exception of the spouse's approval requirement, found all of them to be constitutional.

Conservatives had viewed *Casey* as an opportunity to overturn *Roe*, and many believed the Court, which include new Republican appointees Justices Clarence Thomas and David Souter, would do so. By affirming *Roe*, however, the Court strengthened *Roe*'s status as a legal precedent, thus giving *Roe* even greater protection from future legal challenges. The addition of two abortion-rights supporters to the Court in the 1990s, Ruth Bader Ginsberg and Stephen Breyer, helped to solidify *Roe* by creating a solid six-justice majority in favor of keeping abortion a fundamental right.

In so doing, the Court acknowledged that *Roe*, at last, had become the legal precedent of the land, and while opponents to the Court's decision in *Casey* were determined to continue their attempts to overturn it, chipping away at the law's provisions a little at a time, their chances for success had grown suddenly slimmer with the Court's 1992 decision.

Stenberg v. Carhart

Since *Casey*, the Court has decided only one *major* abortion case, a challenge to a Nebraska law banning what opponents call the "partial birth" abortion procedure. The term, partial birth, refers to a medical procedure known as "dilation and extraction" (D&X). It's a procedure that involves terminating the pregnancy by partially extracting the fetus from the uterus, collapsing its skull, and removing its brain—thus destroying it.

This procedure is usually performed late in the second trimester, between the 20th and 24th weeks of pregnancy.

In 2000, the Supreme Court agreed to hear the case of *Stenberg v. Carhart*, which challenged the constitutionality of partial birth abortion and the Nebraska law that provided that doctors or others found guilty of violating the law were subject to a fine and jail time. The law also provided that a doctor convicted of violating the law would lose his or her state license to practice medicine.

In a 5-4 decision, the Court ruled that the Nebraska law had violated the Constitution as interpreted in *Casey* and also in *Roe*. Justice Breyer, delivering the majority opinion for the Court, stated that the statute lacked the requisite exception "for the preservation of the … health of the mother." Citing *Casey*, Breyer determined that the state has a responsibility to promote but not to endanger a woman's health while regulating acceptable methods of abortion.

In addition, the majority in *Stenberg* found the wording of the Nebraska law unclear, because it could be interpreted by doctors to include not only the D&X procedure but other abortion methods as well. The Court majority ruled that this ambiguity imposed an "undue burden" on a woman's ability to choose an abortion, as well as on all those who perform partial birth abortion procedures while fearing prosecution, conviction, and imprisonment.

The vote was unexpectedly close for a court in which support for the basic right to abortion was expected to receive six votes. In a surprising last-minute shift, Justice Kennedy dissented from the majority, emphasizing what he described as the "consequential moral difference" between the dilation and extraction method and other abortion procedures.

The Court's decision reversed previous bans on D&X abortions in more than thirty different states. But working with Congress to pass a new more restrictive *federal* law, President George W. Bush signed in 2003 the first federal act banning partial birth abortions. Abortion rights advocates immediately challenged the federal government, and the lower courts, citing *Stenberg*, struck it down. However, the federal government gave notice of appeal and eventually won the cases.

"Jane Roe" Goes Back to Court

In 2004, in an ironic and surprising reversal, Norma McCorvey (Jane Roe, the plaintiff in 1973's groundbreaking *Roe v. Wade*) filed a motion with the US District Court in Dallas to have the *Roe* case overturned. In doing so, she asked the court to consider new evidence that abortion hurts women. Included in her filings were affidavits from more than a thousand women who said they had regretted having had their abortions. For McCorvey, the journey from abortion advocate to abortion foe had been long and winding.

In 1970, Norma McCorvey was described as a pregnant woman who "wished to terminate her pregnancy by an abortion 'performed by a competent, licensed physician, under safe, clinical conditions'; … was unable to get a 'legal' abortion in Texas," and the case focused on the idea that "the Texas statutes were unconstitutionally vague and that they abridged her right of personal privacy … "[1]

But the *true* story, as Norma McCorvey later explained it, was nowhere near what had been portrayed in court. A woman who was relatively ignorant of the facts of her own case, McCorvey claimed that her attorneys used her for their own predetermined ends. They "were looking for somebody, anybody, to use to further their own agenda. I was their most willing dupe."[2]

After becoming pregnant with her second child, she sought to end her pregnancy. She was not aware of all the implications of abortion or even what the term meant. "Abortion to me," she said, "meant 'going back' to the condition of not being pregnant."[3] She did not realize that the process would end a human life. She said that her attorney, Sarah Weddington, rather than correcting her misconceptions, merely confused the issue: "For their part, my lawyers lied to me about the nature of abortion. Weddington convinced me, 'It's just a piece of tissue. You just missed your period.'"[4] Another problem was that Norma claimed that her pregnancy was the result of a gang-rape in order to present a more sympathetic picture. That, as she has since confessed, was untrue.[5]

McCorvey has long admitted that her actual involvement in the case was minimal. She had signed the initial affidavit without ever reading it, and "was never invited into court. I never testified. I was never present before any court on any level, and I was never at any hearing on my case … I found out about the decision from the newspaper just like the rest of the country."[6]

Even though she had spearheaded the pro-choice movement and its goal of opening up the right to legalized abortion to women, Norma McCorvey never experienced the abortion procedure. Instead, she delivered her baby and gave it up for adoption.[7]

After hearing the evidence presented by McCorvey to overturn *Roe*, a three-judge panel of the Fifth US Circuit Court of Appeals in New Orleans dismissed Norma McCorvey's motion on November 14, 2004. McCorvey had claimed that she had new information that would affect the 1973 case. The lower court disagreed, and the Supreme Court denied review of the case.

McCorvey, who seven years earlier had founded the pro-life organization "Roe No More," an outreach group formed to legislate for the overturn of *Roe*, disbanded the group in 2008 but continues her fight against abortion.

Gonzales v. Carhart

Three years after the appeals court dismissal of McCorvey's motion, the Supreme Court heard arguments in a case entitled *Gonzales v. Carhart*. It concerned the previously mentioned Partial-Birth Abortion Ban Act of 2003, which George W. Bush had signed into law. Pro-life supporters referred to it simply as "partial-birth abortion." In the law, Congress had provided that anyone found in violation would receive a prison sentence of up to 2.5 years. In its 2007 decision, the Supreme Court upheld the ban against partial-birth abortion by a narrow 5-4 majority. The decision marked the first time the Court had allowed a ban on *any* form of abortion since the landmark *Roe v. Wade*. The majority opinion, which was written by Justice Anthony Kennedy, was joined by Justices Antonin Scalia, Clarence Thomas, and two of the more recent appointees to the Court, Justice Samuel Alito and Chief Justice John Roberts.

Encouraged by the decision in *Carhart,* a number of state legislatures quickly stepped up their efforts to limit access to abortion by weakening the Court's ruling in *Roe.* Ten states—Alabama, Arizona, Florida, Kansas, Louisiana, Mississippi, North Carolina, Oklahoma, Texas, and Virginia—enacted laws that require physicians to perform an ultrasound procedure before performing an abortion. In addition, a number of states have recently passed laws that, with very few exceptions, outlaw abortion beginning at twenty weeks into pregnancy, instead of the previous norm of twenty-four.

Other recent laws, requiring ultrasounds prior to an abortion, sprang from the Supreme Court's 1992 decision in *Casey,* in which the Court upheld a state regulation requiring patients to give "informed consent" at least twenty-four hours before having an abortion. The new ultrasound laws create a more demanding consent requirement by requiring women seeking abortions to undergo a trans-vaginal ultrasound procedure first. Some of the new laws also require that the woman see an image of the fetus and listen to the sound of its heartbeat prior to receiving an abortion.

Not surprisingly, pro-choice advocates found such actions to be intrusive and have challenged them in federal court. In *Texas Medical Providers Performing Abortion Services v. Lakey*, a federal district court ruled in August 2011 that the Texas ultrasound law interfered with the First Amendment rights of physicians and patients to privacy. In January 2012, the Fifth US Circuit Court of Appeals reversed that decision, ruling that the compulsory ultrasound laws neither violated the First Amendment nor imposed an "undue burden" on women seeking an abortion.

In another challenge (*Stuart v. Huff*), a federal district court in December 2011 ruled that North Carolina's compulsory ultrasound law, which is similar to the one in Texas, violated the First Amendment rights of physicians and patients; the district court then issued a preliminary injunction barring enforcement of the law. In January 2013, the court upheld the compulsory ultrasound law.

"Fetal Pain" Laws

In another attempt to blunt the decision in *Roe*, nine states—Alabama, Arizona, Georgia, Idaho, Indiana, Kansas, Louisiana, Nebraska, and North Carolina—have enacted laws that prohibit abortions at twenty weeks or later. These laws are based in part on a theory that a fetus, from twenty weeks onward, can experience pain from an abortion procedure. Those who support the theory claim that a twenty-week-old fetus has developed pain sensors and will react to stimuli, such as a needle, with increases in blood pressure, heart rate, and stress hormones—all symptoms of experienced pain.

The doctors and pro-choice groups that oppose such laws insist that the scientific evidence does not support the "fetal pain" theory. They maintain that a fetus does not develop the neurological structures necessary to experience pain until at least twenty-six weeks of development. They argue that prohibiting abortions at twenty weeks in age restricts the right of a mother to terminate the birth before the point of fetal viability. They assert that abortions should be allowed if the pregnancies threaten women's health or involve severe abnormalities in the fetuses. They claim that, while roughly half of all fetuses can survive outside the womb at twenty-four weeks' gestation, there are no known cases of fetal survival before twenty-one weeks.

Knowing this, Arizona enacted an especially tough fetal pain law, barring abortions at twenty weeks, measured from the first day of the pregnant woman's last menstrual period. The law allows exceptions only in cases in which continuation of the pregnancy presents a severe risk of either death or irreversible health impairment to the mother. A group of abortion providers in Arizona challenged the law in federal court, but in July 2012, a federal district court refused to block the law's enforcement. The district court judge in the case, *Isaacson v. Horne*, found that credible scientific evidence supported the state legislature's judgment that a fetus of at least twenty weeks' development can experience pain. The judge also found that mid-pregnancy abortions present higher health risks to women than earlier ones, and that the state's interests in protecting fetuses and women justified the prohibition.

The laws prohibiting abortions at twenty weeks conflict with Supreme Court rulings on when abortions may be banned (beginning at the point of fetal viability, according to the Supreme Court's rulings in both *Roe* and *Casey*). For this reason, circuit courts seem likely to strike down laws to the contrary. On the other hand, *Carhart* signaled the high court's willingness to rethink important premises in this ongoing legal debate, so it would not be surprising if the Supreme Court eventually takes up the issues raised by this new restriction on the availability of abortions in the second trimester of pregnancy.

Problems in Determining "Abortion"

One of the most persistent and troubling aspects of the legal abortion system currently in place is the difficulty in determining when the fetus is "viable" outside the womb. That is, at what point from its conception does the fetus have a "life" of its own (and therefore is subject to protection by the state). In the majority opinion delivered by the Court in *Roe v. Wade*, viability was defined as "potentially able to live outside the mother's womb, even if artificial aid is required. Viability is usually placed at about seven months (28 weeks) but may occur earlier—even as early as 24 weeks." When the court handed down its ruling in *Roe* in 1973, the medical technology of the day suggested that viability could occur as early as at twenty-four weeks, but medical advances over the past three decades have allowed fetuses that are a few weeks less than twenty-four weeks old to survive outside the mother's womb. These scientific achievements, while life-saving for premature babies, have made the legal determination of being "viable" more complicated for the Court.

At only twenty-one weeks and six days from the time of conception, a girl born in 2006 in a Miami, Florida, hospital became the youngest living premature baby in the United States.[8] Because federal laws are different from state laws, legal access to abortion differs among the states. Even within a state, women may have a hard time accessing abortion services, with 87 percent of all US counties having no abortion providers available to them.[9]

Not surprisingly, the legality of abortion in the United States has become a growing political nightmare. Abortion has become a major issue in nomination battles for the US Supreme Court, although nominees as a rule remain silent on the issue during their confirmation hearings, because it is an issue that may one day come before them as sitting justices.

In the meantime, the jockeying in Congress over representatives' positions on abortion continues, just as it does in our nation's courts. As it stands now, abortion is legal in the United States—with a number of exceptions. Depending upon the judges and justices considering the question, those exceptions continuously grow and shrink with changes in the political climate.

Who exerts the most influence over our courts, The pro-life advocates or the pro-choice lobby? That, for today at least, is a question that is virtually impossible to answer. So, the jockeying by our legal system to provide the most widely available, humanly considerate, and morally acceptable solution to a woman's right to privacy in controlling her own body remains in flux.

Perhaps time will tell where the gavel on the question will eventually fall.

Questions to Consider

1. What is *Roe v. Wade*?

2. In which state did *Roe* originate?

3. What was Roe's real name?

4. Which Amendment was used in the *Roe* decision?

5. What in effect did the *Roe v. Wade* decision state?

6. In what year was the *Roe* decision made?

7. Which Amendment in the *Roe* decision gives the right to privacy?

8. Who was "Wade"?

9. What was the court's final vote in *Roe v. Wade?*

Primary Source Documents

The majority opinion, written by Justice Blackmun, defined the following.

1. While 28 U.S.C. § 1253 authorizes no direct appeal to this Court from the grant or denial of declaratory relief alone, review is not foreclosed when the case is properly before the Court on appeal from specific denial of injunctive relief and the arguments as to both injunctive and declaratory relief are necessarily identical. P. 123.

2. Roe has standing to sue; the Does and Hallford do not. Pp. 123-129.

    (a) Contrary to appellee's contention, the natural termination of Roe's pregnancy did not moot her suit. Litigation involving pregnancy, which is "capable of repetition, yet evading review," is an exception to the usual federal rule that an actual controversy [p114] must exist at review stages, and not simply when the action is initiated. Pp. 124-125.

    (b) The District Court correctly refused injunctive, but erred in granting declaratory relief to Hallford, who alleged no federally protected right not assertable as a defense against the good faith state prosecutions pending against him. *Samuels v. Mackell*, 401 U.S. 66. Pp. 125-127.

(c) The Does' complaint, based as it is on contingencies, any one or more of which may not occur, is too speculative to present an actual case or controversy. Pp. 127-129.

3. State criminal abortion laws, like those involved here, that except from criminality only a life-saving procedure on the mother's behalf without regard to the stage of her pregnancy and other interests involved violate the Due Process Clause of the Fourteenth Amendment, which protects against state action the right to privacy, including a woman's qualified right to terminate her pregnancy. Though the State cannot override that right, it has legitimate interests in protecting both the pregnant woman's health and the potentiality of human life, each of which interests grows and reaches a "compelling" point at various stages of the woman's approach to term. Pp. 147-164.

(a) For the stage prior to approximately the end of the first trimester, the abortion decision and its effectuation must be left to the medical judgment of the pregnant woman's attending physician. Pp. 163-164.

(b) For the stage subsequent to approximately the end of the first trimester, the State, in promoting its interest in the health of the mother, may, if it chooses, regulate the abortion procedure in ways that are reasonably related to maternal health. Pp. 163-164.

(c) For the stage subsequent to viability the State, in promoting its interest in the potentiality of human life, may, if it chooses, regulate, and even proscribe, abortion except where necessary, in appropriate medical judgment, for the preservation of the life or health of the mother. Pp. 163-164; 164-165.

4. The State may define the term "physician" to mean only a physician currently licensed by the State, and may proscribe any abortion by a person who is not a physician as so defined. P. 165.

5. It is unnecessary to decide the injunctive relief issue, since the Texas authorities will doubtless fully recognize the Court's ruling [p115] that the Texas criminal abortion statutes are unconstitutional. P. 166.

Blackmun delivered the opinion of the Court, in which Burger, Douglas, Brennan, Stewart, Marshall, and Powell joined.

Byron White was the senior dissenting justice, with Justice Rehnquist concurring. Justices White and Rehnquist wrote emphatic dissenting opinions. White wrote:

"I find nothing in the language or history of the Constitution to support the Court's judgment. The Court simply fashions and announces a new constitutional right for pregnant women and, with scarcely any reason or authority for its action, invests that right with sufficient substance to override most existing state abortion statutes. The upshot is that the people and the legislatures of the 50 States are constitutionally disentitled to weigh the relative importance of the continued existence and development of the fetus, on the one hand, against a spectrum of possible impacts on the woman, on the other hand. As an exercise of raw judicial power, the Court perhaps has authority to do what it does today; but, in my view, its judgment is an improvident and extravagant exercise of the power of judicial review that the Constitution extends to this Court."

White asserted that the Court "values the convenience of the pregnant mother more than the continued existence and development of the life or potential life that she carries." Though he suggested that he "might agree" with the Court's values and priorities, he wrote that he saw "no constitutional warrant for imposing such an order of priorities on the people and legislatures of the States." White criticized the Court for involving itself in the issue of abortion by creating "a constitutional barrier to state efforts to protect human life and by investing mothers and doctors with the constitutionally protected right to exterminate it." He would have left this issue, for the most part, "with the people and to the political processes the people have devised to govern their affairs."

Rehnquist elaborated on several of White's points, asserting that the Court's historical analysis was flawed:

"To reach its result, the Court necessarily has had to find within the scope of the Fourteenth Amendment a right that was apparently completely unknown to the drafters of the Amendment. As early as 1821, the first state law dealing directly with abortion was enacted by the Connecticut Legislature. By the time of the adoption of the Fourteenth Amendment in 1868, there were at least 36 laws enacted by state or territorial legislatures limiting abortion. While many States have amended or updated their laws, 21 of the laws on the books in 1868 remain in effect today."

From this historical record, Rehnquist concluded, "There apparently was no question concerning the validity of this provision or of any of the other state statutes when the Fourteenth Amendment was adopted." Therefore, in his view, "the drafters did not intend to have the Fourteenth Amendment withdraw from the States the power to legislate with respect to this matter."

Chronology

January 1970 Seeking a legal abortion, Norma McCorvey (aka Jane Roe), twenty-one years of age, files a lawsuit against defendant District Attorney Henry Wade in Texas' Dallas County District Court. The Texas court rules in Roe's favor.

December 1971 Defendant Henry Wade files an appeal of the decision of the district court, sending the case into its first round of US Supreme Court arguments.

October 1972 Due to the fact that two recent Nixon appointees—Justices Lewis Powell and William H. Rehnquist—had recently been approved by Congress and appointed to the Supreme Court, the case was scheduled for reargument at a later date.

January 1973 The case of *Roe v. Wade*, 410 U.S. 113, was finally decided in the Supreme Court by a 7-2 majority. The court held that, under the Fourteenth Amendment, most US abortion laws are unconstitutional. Specifically, the court held that until the fetus is "viable" (or able to live outside the mother's womb, a development usually occurring between twenty-four and twenty-eight weeks), a woman can have an abortion for any reason she sees fit.

1976 In *Planned Parenthood of Central Missouri v. Danforth*, the Supreme Court declares a statute that requires parental and spousal consent for abortions unconstitutional.

Congress enacts the Hyde Amendment for the first time, banning the use of federal funds for abortion except in cases of rape, incest or endangerment of the mother's life. This amendment has been attached to the congressional appropriations bill and approved by Congress every year since then.

1983 In *Akron v. Akron Center for Reproductive Health*, the Supreme Court declares unconstitutional an Ohio law that requires all abortions after the first trimester be performed at a hospital, a twenty-four-hour waiting period, and parental consent for girls younger than fifteen.

1989 The Supreme Court deals a blow to anti-abortion forces in *Webster v. Reproductive Health Services* by striking down a law that requires doctors to test the viability of the fetus before performing any abortion. Three justices said they would allow restrictions on abortion but only if the restrictions had a rational basis.

1992 Supporters on either side of the abortion issue are left confused after the Supreme Court rules on *Planned Parenthood of Southeastern Pennsylvania v. Casey*. The court says abortion regulations that present an "undue burden" on women's constitutional right will be prohibited; critics say "undue burden" is too vague.

1994 President Bill Clinton signs the Abortion-Clinic Protection Bill into law, which is designed to protect abortion clinics from attacks, blockades and acts of intimidation by pro-life protesters.

2000 The Food and Drug Administration approves the abortion pill RU-486. The drug enables a woman to terminate a pregnancy within seven weeks from her last menstrual period, without the need for a surgical abortion.

2003 President George W. Bush signs the Partial-Birth Abortion Ban Act, outlawing the procedure known as intact dilation and extraction (D&X). Federal judges quickly issue injunctions that temporarily nullify the law's effect for many abortion providers.

2004 About 800,000 demonstrators gather in Washington for the "March for Women's Lives," a protest against Bush's reproductive rights policies. This is the largest abortion-rights demonstration since a 1992 rally that drew at least 500,000 participants.

2007 The Supreme Court upholds the partial-birth abortion law 5-4 in the first federal restriction on a particular abortion method since *Roe v. Wade*.

In a bitter dissent read from the bench, Justice Ruth Bader Ginsburg says the majority's opinion "cannot be understood as anything other than an effort to chip away a right declared again and again by this court."

2009 President Barack Obama ends a ban on the use of US foreign aid funds by international family planning programs that provided abortions or advice on obtaining one. The ban had first been instituted in 1984 by President Ronald Reagan.

2011 Voters in Mississippi reject the "Personhood" Amendment, which would have outlawed all forms of abortion, including for cases of rape, incest and life-threatening pregnancies.

Chapter Notes

Chapter 1. Dallas, Texas

1. Marian Faux, *Roe v. Wade* (New York, NY: New American Library, 1988), pp. 6–8.

2. Barbara Milbaucr, *The Law Giveth: Legal Aspects of the Abortion Controversy* (New York, NY: Atheneum, 1983), pp. 12–13.

3. Fred W. Friendl and Martha J. H. Elliot, *The Constitution: That Delicate Balance* (New York, NY: Random House, 1984), p. 202.

4. Kristin Luker, *Abortion and the Politics of Motherhood* (Los Angeles, CA: University of California Press, 1984), pp. 50–51.

5. Steven Holmes, *Time*, January 23, 1989, p. 55.

6. Joseph Bell, "A Landmark Decision," *Good Housekeeping*, June 1973, pp. 78–79.

Chapter 2. The "Normalization" of Abortion

1. *Washington Post*, January 25, 1973, p. A5.

2. Marian Faux, *Roe v. Wade* (New York, NY: New American Library, 1988), p. 17.

3. Ibid., p. 18.

4. Joseph Bell, "A Landmark Decision," *Good Housekeeping*, June 1973, p. 148.

5. Sarah Weddington, *A Question of Choice* (New York, NY: G. P. Putnam's Sons, 1992), pp. 51–53.

Chapter 3. A Case for "Jane Roe"

1. Sarah Weddington, *A Question of Choice* (New York, NY: G. P. Putnam's Sons, 1992), p. 14.

2. Ibid., pp. 14–15.

3. Marian Faux, *Roe v. Wade* (New York, NY: New American Library, 1988), p. 74.

4. Ibid.

5. Norman D. Redlich, "Are There 'Certain Rights … Retained by the People'?" *New York University Law Review No. 787*, 1962.

6. *Griswold v. Connecticut* (Majority Opinion), pp. 480–486.

7. Maureen Harrison and Steve Gilbert, eds., *Landmark Decisions of the United States Supreme Court Vol. 1* (Beverly Hills, CA: Excellent Books, 1991), p. 66.

8. Weddington, p. 62.

9. Harrison and Gilbert, p. 67.

Chapter 4. A Case for Henry Wade

1. *Roe v. Wade: The Complete Text of the Official U.S. Supreme Court Decision,* annotated by Bo Schambelan (Philadelphia, PA: Running Press, 1992), p. viii.

2. Marian Faux, *Roe v. Wade* (New York, NY: New American Library, 1988), pp. 102–103.

3. Sarah Weddington, *A Question of Choice* (New York, NY: G. P. Putnam's Sons, 1992), p. 62.

4. Faux, pp. 132–133.

5. Weddington, pp. 65–66.

6. *Roe v. Wade* (Oral Argument Before Statutory Three-Judge United States District Court for Northern District of Texas, July 30, 1970), pp. 75–100.

7. Ibid.

8. Faux, p. 157.

Chapter 5. To the Supreme Court

1. Thomas M. Emerson, "Nine Justices in Search of a Doctrine," *Michigan Law Review No. 64*, December 1965, p. 227.

2. Marian Faux, *Roe v. Wade* (New York, NY: New American Library, 1988), p. 160.

3. *Roe v. Wade: The Complete Text of the Official U.S. Supreme Court Decision,* annotated by Bo Schambelan (Philadelphia, PA: Running Press, 1992), p. viii.

4. *Dallas Morning News,* June 19, 1970, pp. 2D, 14A.

5. *Roe v. Wade,* Schambelan, p. viii.

6. Mark Curriden, *ABA Journal,* July 1989, p. 26.

7. Sarah Weddington, *A Question of Choice* (New York, NY: G. P. Putnam's Sons, 1992), pp. 106–108.

8. Ibid., p. 234.

9. Ibid., p. 239.

10. *Roe v. Wade* (Supreme Court of the United States Oral Arguments, No. 70-18, December 13, 1971), pp. 15–16.

11. Ibid., p. 16.

12. Ibid., p. 31.

13. Ibid., p. 39.

14. Ibid., p. 40.

15. Ibid., p. 44.

16. Ibid., pp. 44–45.

17. Ibid., p. 48.

Chapter 6. Return Engagement

1. Marian Faux, *Roe v. Wade* (New York, NY: New American Library, 1988), p. 277.

2. Ibid.

3. Ibid.

4. Ibid., pp. 284–286.

5. Bob Woodward and Scott Armstrong, *The Brethren: Inside the Supreme Court* (New York, NY: Simon & Schuster, 1979), pp. 180–183.

6. Ibid., pp. 186, 192.

7. Ibid., pp. 186–189; *Time*, February 5, 1973, p. 51.

8. *Roe v. Wade* (Supreme Court of the United States Oral Arguments, No. 70-18, October 11, 1972), pp. 14–15.

9. Ibid., p. 15.

10. Ibid., pp. 20–21.

11. Ibid., p. 20.

12. Ibid.

13. Ibid.

14. Ibid., pp. 21–22.

15. Faux, pp. 253–256.

16. *Roe v. Wade* (Oral Arguments), p. 23.

17. Ibid.

18. Ibid., p. 24.

19. Ibid.

20. Ibid.

21. Ibid., pp. 37–38.

Chapter 7. Settling In

1. Sarah Weddington, *A Question of Choice* (New York, NY: G. P. Putnam's Sons, 1992), pp. 145–146.

2. *Roe v. Wade: The Complete Text of the Official U.S. Supreme Court Decision,* annotated by Bo Schambelan (Philadelphia, PA: Running Press, 1992), pp. 13–14.

3. Ibid., p. 18.

4. Ibid., pp. 38–43.

5. Marian Faux, *Roe v. Wade* (New York, NY: New American Library, 1988), p. 313.

6. Fred W. Friendl and Martha J. H. Elliot, *The Constitution: That Delicate Balance* (New York, NY: Random House, 1984), p. 207.

7. Ibid.

Chapter 8. Settling Down

1. Andrea Sachs, *Time*, May 1, 1989, p. 59.

2. *Akron v. Akron Center for Reproductive Health*, 462 U.S. 416 (1983).

3. Fred Barnes, "Reagan's Full-Court Press," *New Republic*, June 10, 1987.

4. Sarah Weddington, *A Question of Choice* (New York, NY: G. P. Putnam's Sons, 1992), p. 205.

5. Richard Lucayo, *Time*, May 1, 1989, p. 22.

6. Andrea Sachs, *Time*, December 5, 1988, p. 60.

7. Ibid.

8. Ibid., p. 58.

9. Steven Holmes, Naushad S. Mehta, and Elizabeth Taylor, *Time*, May 1, 1989, p. 24.

10. Mark Curriden, *ABA Journal*, July 1989, p. 26.

11. Ibid.

12. Weddington, p. 226.

13. Ibid., p. 227.

Chapter 9. The Making of a Precedent

1. *Roe v. Wade*, 410 U.S. 113 (1973), p. 120.

2. Norma McCorvey's testimony before Congress in 1998. See: "The 25th Anniversary of *Roe v. Wade*: Has it Stood the Test of Time?:" Hearing before the Subcommittee on the Constitution, Federalism, and Property Rights of the Senate Judiciary Committee, 105th Congress, 2nd Session (January 21, 1998).

3. Affidavit of Norma McCorvey (June 11, 2003), in *McCorvey v. Hill* (US District Court for the Northern District of Texas, Dallas Division, Civil Action No. 3-3690-B and No. 3-3691-C).

4. Ibid.

5. See Norma McCorvey's testimony before Congress in 1998 as well as her testimony at the 2005 hearing, "The Consequences of *Roe v. Wade* and *Doe v. Bolton*:" Hearing before the Subcommittee on the Constitution of the Senate Judiciary Committee, 109th Congress, 1st Session (June 23, 2005).

6. Affidavit of Norma McCorvey, in *McCorvey v. Hill*.

7. Ibid.

8. Amanda Cable, "The Tiniest Survivor: How the 'Miracle' Baby Born Two Weeks Before the Legal Abortion Limit Clung to Life Against All Odds," *DailyMail.com*, May 22, 2008, http://www.dailymail.co.uk/femail/article-1021034/The-tiniest-survivor-How-miracle-baby-born-weeks-legal-abortion-limit-clung-life-odds.html.

9. "Unequal Access to Abortion," National Abortion Federation, undated, http://prochoice.org/education-and-advocacy/about-abortion/unequal-access-to-abortion/.

Glossary

abortion A deliberate termination of pregnancy.

abortionist A person (who legally should be a doctor) who terminates pregnancies.

affidavit Written declaration made under oath; a written statement sworn to be true before someone legally authorized to administer an oath.

appellant The person who applies for an appeal; opposed to appellee.

appellee The defendant in an appeal; opposed to appellant.

argument A fact or assertion offered as evidence that something is true.

declaratory relief A judge's determination (called a "declaratory judgment") of the parties' rights under a contract or a statute often requested (prayed for) in a lawsuit over a contract.

dilation and extraction Dilatation of the cervix uteri followed by a scraping of the brain for removal.

fetus An unborn or unhatched vertebrate in the later stages of development showing the main recognizable features of the mature human being.

gestation period The time period during which female mammals carry their developing young in utero before birth, beginning with fertilization.

injunction A judicial remedy issued in order to prohibit a party from performing or continuing to perform a certain activity.

legal pleadings Every legal document filed in a lawsuit, petition, motion, and/or hearing, including complaint, petition, answer, demurrer, motion, declaration, and memorandum of points and authorities.

opinion The legal document stating the reasons for a judicial decision.

preliminary injunction A court order made in the early stages of a lawsuit or petition which prohibits the parties from performing an act which is in dispute, thereby maintaining the status quo until there is a final judgment after trial.

pro-choice In favor of abortion.

pro-life Against abortion.

rape To force someone to have intercourse against their will.

standing The right to file a lawsuit or file a petition under the circumstances. A plaintiff will have standing to sue in federal court if a) there is an actual controversy, b) a federal statute gives the federal court jurisdiction, and c) the parties are residents of different states or otherwise fit the constitutional requirements for federal court jurisdiction.

trimester A period of three months; especially one of the three three-month periods into which human pregnancy is divided.

ultrasound Very high frequency sound; used in ultrasonography.

viability The age at which a fetus is potentially able to live outside the mother's womb, even though artificial aid is required.

Further Reading

Books

Forsythe, Clarke. *Abuse of Discretion: The Inside Story of Roe v. Wade.* New York, NY: Encounter Books, 2013.

Hoffer, Peter Charles, and N. E. H. Hull. *Roe v. Wade: The Abortion Rights Controversy in American History, 2nd Edition (Landmark Law Cases and American Society).* Revised. Lawrence, KS: University Press of Kansas, 2010.

McCorvey, Norma, and Andy Meisler. *I Am Roe: My Life, Roe v. Wade, and Freedom of Choice.* Reprint. New York, NY: Perennial, 1995.

Rafferty, Phillip A. *Roe v. Wade: Unraveling the Fabric of America.* Revised, Expanded. Mustang, OK: Tate Publishing, 2013.

Resler, Roger. *Compelling Interest: The Real Story Behind Roe v. Wade.* Cleveland, OH: eChristian Books, 2012.

Weddington, Sarah. *A Question of Choice.* New York, NY: G.P. Putnam's Sons, 1992.

Websites

Cornell University Law School

www.law.cornell.edu/supremecourt/text/410/113

Complete *Roe v. Wade* Court Syllabus, Opinion, and Dissent

Landmark Cases of the US Supreme Court

www.landmarkcases.org/en/landmark/home

In-depth analyses of *Roe v. Wade* and other landmark Supreme Court cases

Oyez IIT Chicago-Kent College of Law

www.oyez.org/cases/1971/70-18

Complete record of *Roe v. Wade* and other landmark cases, including audio files of Court proceedings where available

Index

Rehnquist, William, 65, 66, 74, 75, 84
"right of privacy," 27, 76, 79, 89, 97
Roberts, John, 99
Roman Catholic Church, 78, 81
Ruby, Jack, 33

S

Scalia, Antonin, 84, 99
Schwartz, Tobiane, 52
Souter, David, 86, 92, 94
Southern Methodist University Law School, 35
Stenberg v. Carhart, 94, 95, 96
Stewart, Potter, 56, 64, 68, 70, 73, 74, 75
Stuart v. Huff, 100

T

Taylor, William McLaughlin, 41
Texas Medical Providers Performing Abortion Services v. Lakey, 100
Third District Court of Appeals, 92
Thomas, Clarence, 99
Thompson v. State, 58
Thornburgh, Dick, 85, 92
Tolle, John, 33, 35, 36, 38, 39, 40, 41, 44, 45

trimester, 14, 15, 73, 74, 76, 77, 83, 90, 92, 93, 95, 102
TRO, 15

U

unconstitutional, 31, 32, 48, 49, 51, 63, 71, 93
"undue burden," 92, 93, 95, 100
University of Notre Dame, 33

V

viability, 77, 79, 80, 85, 93, 101, 102, 103

W

Wade, Henry, 31, 33, 35, 36, 37, 45, 51, 54
Warren, Earl, 27
Weddington, Ron, 24, 25, 66
White, Byron, 56, 63, 66, 67, 68, 74, 75, 87
White House, 82, 83
Willke, John, 85

Y

Yale University, 26

Z

"zone of privacy," 27, 29